Pray Strategy Resource Book

By
Ruth Shinness

This book is put together with
Scriptural skills that
"Unlock the Heavens"
And brings to earth the good that
God has always planned
For you and yours.

OTHER BOOKS
Books are published in Russian, Korean, and French

PRAYER STRATEGY RESOURCE BOOK: Individual topics for each page. Pick out what you need or desire. Jesus has already won it all for you and is waiting to activate it into your life and the lives of others. Large size 8x11.5, 80 pages. Small size 5.5x8, 80 pages.

UNLOCKING THE HEAVENS: Step by step story of how Ruth learned scriptural strategy to *Unlock the Heavens* for her and her prayer needs and the joy of seeing answers spring forth.

MIRACLE FAMILY PRAYER BOOK: Families agreeing together in prayer, allowing them to flourish in God's love and blessing. A page for each day, simple, taking a few minutes a day. 5x7 Pamphlet

PRAYING IN YOUR FUTURE: Let God unfold the future He has planned for you. Prayer focus for each day of the week, or you can pray the whole book, or pick and choose what you want. 5x7 Pamphlet

PRAYING FOR YOUR CITY: A prayer page for each day. Believing prayers of great joy for city revival. Pray the blessings of the Lord on your city. Get others to pray with you. There is power in the prayer of agreement. 5x7 Pamphlet.

FEAR NOT: Jewish prayer book, 4"x51/2" with 18 pages. Scriptures from Jewish Scripture books. Prayers that bring peace and comfort in the midst of fear and uncertainty.

LIVING WATERS: CASSETTE TAPE Ruth's voice doing the prayers. Sons David playing the clarinet and Tom playing the guitar for background for the prayers. Inspirational, bringing you into the Lord's presence, praying along with God's Word.

PRAYING IN YOUR FUTURE: CASSETTE TAPE Ruth's voice doing the prayers from the Praying In Your Future Book. Son Tom playing different stringed instruments with lovely arrangements of hymns in background.

SCRIPTURAL PRAYERS WITH MUSIC: CD, containing the two cassettes above.

UNLOCKING THE HEAVENS DVD SEMINAR Four hours long, Four Topics.

To obtain additional copies of this material, please write or call or email
Ruth Shinness-Brinduse
2539 E. 450 N. Anderson, IN 46012-9518
Email: PrayerStrategy@juno.com Web page: www.prayerstrategy.com
Phone: (765) 643-0612 & (765)-642-0623

Publisher Evangel Press

TABLE OF CONTENTS

Ruth Shinness 2539 E. 450 N. Anderson, IN 46012   Web: www.prayerstrategy.com
e-mail PrayerStrategy@juno.com Phone (765) 643-0612 & (765) 642-0623

1

HOW I LEARNED TO PRAY THE ANSWERS

In 1970, I began to spend my days praying and studying scriptures. By 1975, instead of having answers, some things in my life got worse, developing into a family crisis.

Why didn't I have answers to my prayers? It was because I didn't have the skills in prayer. I read all the books I could on prayer, but they did not give me the help I needed.

My first Prayer Strategy insights came when I started going to a church where they taught me the power of praying the scriptures. I got busy finding and praying scripture. Five years later, I had many answers from "reminding God of His promises." Isaiah. 62:6 AMP.

The family sorrow was turned to joy when the loved one gave his heart to the Lord. I myself was healed of a physical problem, delivered of a spirit of fear, and saw many answers from this way of prayer. It took over four years before these answers started to manifest.

Next, I was to learn a strategy to bring in the answers more quickly. In 1991, another big crisis arose in my life because of my husband's health. I decided I would gather scriptures to pray for the situation. When I started to do that, the verse Mark 11:24 NIV *"Therefore I tell you, whatever you ask for in prayer, believe that you have received it, and it will be yours."* loomed big in my mind. If I believed that I received my answer when I prayed, then I could be sure that I had what I was praying for. I had never believed that I had my answer at the time I had prayed. I was an unbeliever in this area. I decided that I would be grateful that God had heard, and that now I received what I had asked for.

It was as if I had taken a dive into the stream of God's blessings. I started seeing answers quickly. These answers kept flowing into my life and over my whole family.

The result of praying the scriptures this way allowed me to abide in the Presence of the Lord more. Now when I prayed with such joy and gratitude, His abiding presence would come into my heart to overwhelm me with His love. I found that I could live in this oasis of love in the midst of the most trying times of my life.

In July of 1995, I taught my four granddaughters between the ages of 8-12 to pray this way. The presence of God came upon them just like it had for me; and they said, "Grandma, can we pray this way when we go home?"

When I took them home I made prayer books for each of the two families with every person having a prayer book. I put a page in for Mother, Father, Children, Prosper, and Family. They prayed one page a day, taking just a few minutes. It was very simple.

Other family members wanted prayer books also. Many scriptural answers started to unfold for our family on a regular basis. What joy!

A time of testing came to one of our families. God was wanting deeper dredges into a pocket of hurt that needed healing. These prayers give rest and His presence at these times of restructuring. Then scriptural answers start to unfold before us.

Other people are now praying these paraphrased scriptures. We are seeing many people encouraged by wonderful answers.

Ruth Shinness 2539 E. 450 N Anderson, IN 46012-9518 Web: www.prayerstrategy.com
e-mail PrayerStrategy@juno.com Phone (765) 643-0612 & (765) 642-0623

TUNING UP YOUR PRAYER LIFE

I saw in the Scriptures that there were five things I was to do day and night: **1. Abide in Me, and I in you.** John 15:4a KJV **2. Be joyful always.** 1Thess.5:16 NIV **3. Pray continually.** 1 Thess. 5:17 NIV **4. Give thanks in all circumstances.** 1 Thess. 5:18 NIV **5. In His law doth he meditate day and night.** Psalm 1:2b KJV.

I would ask myself these following questions: How could I do five different things at one time? How could I meditate on the Word of God and pray at the same time? How could I be joyful always and pray the concerns I have. How could I abide in the Lord and meditate on Scripture at the same time? How could I be thankful about everything as I prayed?

When I put my prayer book together, I realized it included all the above. This combination is the secret to *Unlocking the Heavens,* wrapping you up in the Glory of the Lord, while good continually flows from the loving Father's hand into your life and the life of others.

HOW TO PRAY THE BOOK

1. I like to pray the bold print. It seems to be even more effective when I pray aloud.
2. As I read the scriptural prayer, I put my mind on the Lord in gratitude and love for the answer I see in this prayer. This attitude unfolds all the areas listed above. My heart is overwhelmed as I meditate on the victory that has already been won for me.
3. Meditate on separate words in the prayers which brings much creative thought to my mind.
4. I think of the joy that others and I have now that we have the promises that Jesus died to give us. I am full of thanksgiving.
5. I believe God has heard me and it is done. This makes me a believer. God calls those things that be not just as though they were really so. I do that also.
6. When I have a special need, I look for the Scriptures that would provide the answer. I meditate on that instead of the problem.
   a. The bigger the concern, the more time I spend seeing the scriptural answers.
   b. The more I abide in Heaven's answers that Jesus already won for me, the more the answers manifest in my earthly realm.
7. The "Forgiving and Blessing" page is important to use daily if needed to keep your spirit free from the sin of unforgiveness and on God's track at all times.
   a. If I have a serious problem with the sin of unforgivness, I pray the prayers often and pray many blessings for that person. I am soon free.
8. I like to soak in the prayers of a certain topic I am interested in for a period of time. The Bible says to meditate on scripture.
9. I am now "joyful in the house of prayer".
10. I spoke to a well-organized prayer group in South Bend. They decided to just take one scripture prayer from the book for each concern and all in the group would agree in prayer with that passage. Matt.18:19 They began to get remarkable answers to prayer. They numbered each prayer, so when they call someone to pray, they just said the page and the number of the prayer. They also find that people who don't have time to pray much will pray one scripture for a concern, rather than a whole page. They encouraged me to number the prayers for easy reference. Testimony Page 74.

Ruth Shinness 2539 E. 450 N. Anderson, IN 46012 Web: www.prayerstrategy.com
e-mail PrayerStrategy@juno.com Phone (765) 643-0612 & (765) 642-0623

3

PRAYER: SCRIPTURAL INSTRUCTION

Psalm 78:32-3 KJV For all this they sinned still and believed not for his wondrous works. Therefore their days did he consume in vanity, and their years in trouble. The purpose of scriptural instruction is to teach strategy on how to believe for His wondrous works.

THE WARFARE IS FOUGHT IN YOUR MIND

11 Corth 10:4-5 AMP (For the weapons of our warfare are not carnal, but mighty through God to the pulling down of strongholds:) casting down imaginations and every high thing that exalted itself against the knowledge of God, and bringing into captivity every thought to the obedience of God. Bring your thoughts to align with what the Word says is already ours or is God's will for us. It is a warfare and not easy.

WHAT TO PUT IN YOUR MIND

1 Thes. 5:16 KJV Rejoice evermore, 17 Pray without ceasing, 18 In everything give thanks. Psalm 1:2 KJV In His law doth he meditate day and night. John 15:4 KJV Abide in me and I in you. It is possible for prayers to contain all the above at the same time for great results.

SAYING THE WORD OF GOD

Isaiah 55:10-11 NIV As the rain and the snow come down from heaven, and do not return to it without watering the earth and making it bud and flourish, so that it yields seed for the sower and bread for the eater, so is my word that goes out from my mouth: It will not return void, but will accomplish what I desire and achieve the purpose for which I sent it. Just as the rain waters the earth, so God's Word going out of our mouth brings forth His desire and purpose.

Isaiah 62:6 AMP I have set watchmen upon your walls, O Jerusalem, who will never hold their peace day or night; you who [are His servants and by your prayers] put the Lord in remembrance [of His promises], keep not silence, and give Him no rest until He establishes Jerusalem and makes it a praise in the earth. How often do you remind God of His promises? Day and night. For how long? Until He establishes that promise.

Mark 11:23 KJV Whosoever shall say to this mountain be thou removed and cast into the sea and shall not doubt in his heart, but shall believe that those things which he says shall come to pass, he shall have whatsoever he says. What we say and continue to say comes to pass and our faith grows as we hear ourselves say it.

Hebrews 10:23 KJV Let us hold fast to our confession of faith without wavering; for he is faithful who promised. Keep on saying it.

Proverbs 18:21 KJV Death and life are in the power of the tongue. The choice is ours to say the words of life or to say the words of death.

BELIEVE IN THE NOW

Mark 11:24 KJV What things soever you desire, when you pray, believe that ye receive them and ye shall have them. We desire what we have requested; now we believe we have received it. We rejoice.

Ruth Shinness 2539 E. 450 N Anderson, IN 46012-9518 Web: www.prayerstrategy.com
e-mail PrayerStrategy@juno.com Phone (765) 643-0612 & (765) 642-0623

Romans 10:9-10 KJV With the heart man believeth unto righteousness; and with the mouth confession is made unto salvation. Scriptural way to receive: Believe in the heart, confess (say) with the mouth. You receive the promises just like you did your salvation.

Matt. 21:22 KJV All things whatsoever ye shall ask in prayer, believing, ye shall receive. We have asked; now we believe that we have received.

1 John 5:14-15 NIV This is the confidence we have in approaching God: that if we ask anything according to his will, he hears us. And if we know that he hears us--whatever we ask--we know that we have what we asked of him. He has heard us and we have it, what is there left to do but to praise Him?

WHAT GOD SAYS

Romans 4:17 KJV God...calleth those things that be not as though they were. We like to call out the problem; God likes to call out the answer.

Hebrews 11:3 KJV The worlds were framed by the word of God. We are co-laborers with Christ. God said the Word to create and we also can say God's word and create.

PRAISE BRINGS THE VICTORY

Romans 4:20 KJV He staggered not at the promise of God through unbelief; but grew strong and was empowered by faith as he gave praise and glory to God, fully satisfied and assured that God was able and mighty to keep his word and do what he had promised. Our part: give praise and glory to God. No begging; it is finished.

Philip. 4:6 NIV Do not be anxious about anything, but in everything, by prayer and petition, with thanksgiving, present your request to God. We are grateful that God has heard and answered--all is in His hands.

Psalm 149:6 KJV Let the high praises of God be in their mouth, and a two edged sword in their hand. The two-edged sword is the Word that we hold before the Lord with our praises to defeat the enemy.

Psalm 67:5-6 KJV Let the people praise thee, O God; let all the people praise thee. Then shall the earth yield her increase; and God, even our own God, shall bless us. You have heard our prayer, O God, and we praise You while You bring forth the wonderful increase You have for us.

Isaiah 56:7 KJV Even them will I bring to my holy mountain, and make them joyful in my house of prayer: their burnt offerings and their sacrifices shall be accepted upon mine altar; for mine house shall be called an house of prayer for all people. Indeed, we are joyful in prayer.

FIND OTHERS TO SPEAK THE SAME THING

Matt 18:19 KJV Verily I say unto you, that if two of you shall agree on earth as touching anything that they shall ask, it shall be done for them by my Father which is in heaven.

Genesis 11:6 AMP Behold, they are of one people, and they have all one language; and this is only the beginning of what they will do: and now nothing they imagined they can do will be impossible to them. There is power of agreement and in saying the same thing.

JOY AND GLADNESS

1. Because I have put my trust in You, You have made me to rejoice. I keep shouting for joy because You defend me. Because I love You, You have filled me with happiness. Psalm 5:11 TLB Make everyone rejoice who puts his trust in you. Keep them shouting for joy because you are defending them. Fill all who love you with your happiness.

2. I have a happy heart, so I have continual joy in Your presence, Lord. Proverbs 15:15 KJV He that is of a merry heart *hath* a continual feast.

3. Holy, Holy, Holy are You Lord of hosts: the whole earth is full of Your Glory. Isaiah 6:3 KJV And one cried unto another, and said, Holy, holy, holy *is* the LORD of hosts: the whole earth *is* full of his glory.

4. With joy, Lord, I draw water from Your wells of salvation. Isaiah 12:3 KJV Therefore with joy shall ye draw water out of the wells of salvation.

5. I say "Thank you for Your kindness" every morning, and every evening I rejoice in all Your faithfulness. You have done so much for me, O Lord, no wonder I am glad. Psalm 92:2 The Book Every morning, tell him, "Thank you for your kindness," and every evening, rejoice in all his faithfulness. Sing his praises, accompanied by music from the harp and lute and lyre. You have done so much for me, O Lord. No wonder I am glad! I sing for joy.

6. Jesus, You have set me free and I come along with singing, and everlasting joy is upon my head. I have obtained joy and gladness, and sorrow and sighing have gone away from me. Isaiah 5:10 KJV And the ransomed of the LORD shall return, and come to Zion with songs and everlasting joy upon their heads: they shall obtain joy and gladness, and sorrow and sighing shall flee away.

7. You have given me a new song to sing of praise unto You, my God. Now many hear the glorious things You have done for me, and stand in awe before You, and put their trust in You. Psalm 40:3 TLB He has given me a new song to sing of praises to our God. Now many will hear of the glorious things he did for me, and stand in awe before the Lord, and put their trust in him.

8. You have come to live among us. You have been mighty to save me. You have given me the victory! You rejoice over me with gladness! You love me and don't accuse me. Is this a choir I hear? No, it is You exulting over me with a happy song. Zeph. 3:17 TLB For the Lord your God has arrived to live among you. He is a mighty Savior. He will give you victory. He will rejoice over you with great gladness; he will love you and not accuse you." Is that a joyous choir I hear? No, it is the Lord himself exulting over you in happy song.

Ruth Shinness 2539 E. 450 N Anderson, IN 46012-9518 Web: www.prayerstrategy.com
e-mail PrayerStrategy@juno.com Phone (765) 643-0612 & (765) 642-0623

PRAISE

1. You are letting me praise You, O God, so now I am yielding my increase and You, my very own God, are blessing me. Psalm 67:5-6 KJV Let the people praise thee, O God; let all the people praise thee. Then shall the earth yield her increase; and God, even our own God, shall bless us.

2. I am praising You with my whole heart. Psalm 9:1a TLB O Lord, I will praise you with all my heart.

3. Lord, I am giving You thank offerings, even when it is a sacrifice. That honors You and prepares the way, so You are showing me more and more of Your salvation. This salvation means liberty, deliverance, prosperity, safety, and saving for me. Psalm 50:23 NIV He who sacrifices thank offerings honors me, and he prepares the way so that I may show him the salvation of God.

4. I am singing praise unto Your name forever; that way, I am able to perform my daily vows. Psalm 61:8 KJV So will I sing praise unto thy name forever, that I may daily perform my vows.

5. Because I seek You, Lord, You are letting me rejoice and be glad in You. I love Your salvation, so I say continually, "Let the Lord be magnified." Psalm 70:4 KJV Let all those that seek thee rejoice and be glad in thee: and let such as love thy salvation say continually, Let God be magnified.

6. O Thank You, Lord. I am through with mourning and a life of ashes, for the beauty of Your spirit is upon me with great joy in my heart. My life is full of praise instead of heaviness. You have planted me like a strong graceful oak for Your glory. Isaiah 61:3 TLB To all who mourn in Israel he will give: Beauty for ashes; Joy instead of mourning; Praise instead of heaviness. For God has planted them like strong and graceful oaks for his own glory.

7. My mouth is filled with Your praise and Your honor all the day. Psalm 71:8 KJV Let my mouth be filled with thy praise and with thy honour all the day.

8. Because I believe Your words are true, I break out with songs of praise. Psalm 106:12 MES Then they believed his words were true and broke out in songs of praise.

9. I am blessed to know the password of praise. I shout in Your bright presence, Lord, delighted to dance all the day long, for I know who You are, what You do--I can't keep it quiet, for Your beauty is inside of me. I am walking on air. Psalm 89:15-17 MES Blessed are the people who know the password of praise, who shout on parade in the bright presence of God. Delighted, they dance all the day long; they know who you are, what you do—they can't keep quiet! Your vibrant beauty has gotten inside of us.

Ruth Shinness 2539 E. 450 N. Anderson, IN 46012 Web: www.prayerstrategy.com
e-mail PrayerStrategy@juno.com Phone (765) 643-0612 & (765) 642-0623

7

PRAYER FOR THOSE IN AUTHORITY

1. We pray for Your highest will for others, Lord, especially for our leaders; and we thank You for all You are doing for them through our prayers. Because of these prayers, we are able to live in peace and quiet, thinking much about You. 1 Timothy 2:1-2 TLB Here are my directions: Pray much for others; plead for God's mercy upon them; give thanks for all he is going to do for them. Pray in this way for kings and all others who are in authority over us, or are in places of high responsibility, so that we can live in peace and quietness, spending our time in godly living and thinking much about the Lord.

2. Our prayer for our leaders is that they now respect and fear You, Lord, so that now they have wisdom and hate the evil of pride, arrogance, corruption, and deceit of every kind. Proverbs 8:13 TLB If anyone respects and fears God, he will hate evil. For wisdom hates pride, arrogance, corruption, and deceit of every kind.

3. We believe that because of our prayers You have turned the thoughts of our leaders' hearts in a way that blesses our country, our city, our churches and our homes. Proverbs 21:1 TLB Just as water is turned into irrigation ditches, so the Lord directs the king's thoughts. He turns them wherever he wants to.

4. We pray for the salvation of our leaders and You have heard our prayers, and now these leaders rejoice in Your salvation with great strength and joy. Psalm 21:1 KJV The king shall joy in thy strength, O LORD; and in thy salvation how greatly shall he rejoice!

5. Because of our prayers, we believe that our leaders have great glory in Your salvation and that You, Lord, have placed honor and majesty upon them. Psalm 21:5 KJV His glory is great in thy salvation: honour and majesty hast thou laid upon him.

6. You, God, have removed the wicked from before our leaders so they are able to rule in a spiritual and moral righteousness in every area and relation. Proverbs 25:5 AMP Take away the wicked from before the king, and his throne will be established in righteousness,.spiritual and moral rectitude in every area and relation.

7. Thank You for cutting off the strength of evil leaders and increasing the power of good men in their place. Psalm 75:10 TLB "I will cut off the strength of evil men," says the Lord, "and increase the power of good men in their place."

8. Lord, I obey those who have the rule over me and submit to them. Hebrews 13:17 KJV Obey them that have the rule over you, and submit yourself.

Ruth Shinness 2539 E. 450 N Anderson, IN 46012-9518 Web: www.prayerstrategy.com
e-mail PrayerStrategy@juno.com Phone (765) 643-0612 & (765) 642-0623

PRAYER FOR THOSE IN AUTHORITY

9. We believe that our leaders have turned about face. You have revised their lives. Look, You are already pouring Your spirit upon them; You tell them all You know. Proverbs 1:23 MES About face! I can revise your life. Look, I'm ready to pour out my spirit on you; I'm ready to tell you all I know.

10. Jesus, You have spoiled the principalities and the powers of the devil and we agree that these powers are now bound over our government, our city, our churches, our ministries and our families. We declare Jesus' Lordship. Col. 2:15 KJV And having spoiled principalities and powers, he made a shew of them openly, triumphing over them in it. 1 John 3:8 KJV For this purpose the Son of God was manifested, that he might destroy the works of the devil.

11. We rejoice that our pastors, church government and people in our churches have repented, that their sins are now blotted out, and that times of refreshing and revival have come from Your presence, Lord. Acts 3:19 KJV Repent ye therefore, and be converted, that your sins may be blotted out, when the times of refreshing shall come from the presence of the Lord.

12. We thank You for raising up godly men and women to rule over us. Psalm 75:6-7 The Book For promotion and power come from nowhere on earth, but only from God. He promotes one and deposes another.

13. Our leaders trust in You, Lord. Your unfailing love keeps them from stumbling. Psalm 21:7 NLT For the king trust in the Lord. The unfailing love of the Most High will keep him from stumbling.

14. We pray that our President lives close to You forever, Lord. We believe You have sent out Your loving kindness and truth to guard and watch over him. Psalm 61:7 TLB And I shall live before the Lord forever. Oh, send your loving-kindness and truth to guard and watch over me.

15. May our President live long. I will pray for him and bless him all the day long. Psalm 72:15 NIV Long may he live! May gold from Sheba be given him. May people ever pray for him and bless him all day long.

16. Thank You for helping our President to judge as You would. You help him give justice to Your people, even to the poor. Psalm 72:1b,2 TLB O God, help the king to judge as you would. Help him to give justice to your people, even to the poor.

Ruth Shinness 2539 E. 450 N. Anderson, IN 46012   Web: www.prayerstrategy.com
e-mail PrayerStrategy@juno.com Phone (765) 643-0612 & (765) 642-0623

9

MY PASTOR

1. Thank You, Lord, that there is no one else so like-minded with me as my pastor. He sincerely cares for me and my state. He is a man that does not seek his own things but the things that are of You, Jesus Christ. Philip. 2:20-21 NKJV For I have no one like-minded, who will sincerely care for your state. For all seek their own, not the things which are of Christ Jesus.

2. My pastor has a proven character and serves well in the Gospel. Philip. 2:22-23 NKJV But you know his proven character, that as a son with *his* father he served with me in the gospel. Therefore I hope to send him at once, as soon as I see how it goes with me.

3. The Word of God is nigh unto this man. It is in his mouth, it is in his heart. He preaches the Word of faith. Romans 10:8: KJV What saith it? The word is nigh thee, *even* in thy mouth, and in thy heart: that is, the word of faith, which we preach.

4. My pastor follows You, Jesus, so You are with him and honor him wherever he goes. John 12:26 KJV If any man serve me, let him follow me; and where I am, there shall also my servant be: if any man serve me, him will my Father honour.

5. My pastor is kind to me, he pleases me, and speaks good words to me; and I will be his servant forever. 2 Chron.10:7 KJV And they spake unto him, saying, If thou be kind to this people, and please them, and speak good words to them, they will be thy servants forever.

6. Thank You, Lord, for giving me a pastor after Your own heart, who feeds me with knowledge and understanding. Jeremiah 3:15 KJV And I will give you pastors according to mine heart, which shall feed you with knowledge and understanding.

7. Thank You, Lord, that You bless my pastor when he comes in a place and when he goes out. Deut. 28:6 TLV Blessings when you come in, Blessings when you go out.

8. Lord, You defeat every enemy that comes against my pastor and the people of my congregation. When the enemy marches against us, Lord, You scatter them before us in seven directions. Deut. 28:7 TLV "The Lord will defeat your enemies before you; they will march out together against you but scatter before you in seven directions!

Ruth Shinness 2539 E. 450 N Anderson, IN 46012-9518 Web: www.prayerstrategy.com
e-mail PrayerStrategy@juno.com Phone (765) 643-0612 & (765) 642-0623

MY PASTOR

9. I am glad my pastor bears good fruit in his ministry and the people of my congregation are healthy in every way. Everyone prospers in everything they do. You have given them the church You planned to bless them in. Deut. 28:8 TLB The Lord will bless you with good crops and healthy cattle, and prosper everything you do when you arrive in the land the Lord your God is giving you.

10. Thank You that You have changed the people of our congregation into a holy people dedicated to You, able to obey You, walking in Your ways. Deut.28:9 TLB He will change you into a holy people dedicated to himself; this he has promised to do if you will only obey him and walk in his ways.

11. All the nations of the world see that my pastor belongs to You, Lord, and they stand in awe of him. Deut. 28:10 TLB All the nations in the world shall see that you belong to the Lord, and they will stand in awe.

12. You have given an abundance of good things into the church You have given me. Deut. 28:11 TLB The Lord will give you an abundance of good things in the land, just as he promised: many children, many cattle, and abundant crops.

13. You have rained down an anointing on him so he bears good fruit in every season. Deut. 28:12a TLB He will open to you his wonderful treasury of rain in the heavens, to give you fine crops every season.

14. God, Thank You for making my pastor an able minister of the New Testament, not of the law but of the spirit. 2 Corth. 3:6 KJV Who (God) also hath made us able ministers of the new testament. Not of the letter, but of the spirit: for the letter killeth, but the spirit giveth life.

15. Lord, You have increased my pastor's greatness and comfort him on every side. Psalm 71:21 KJV Thou shalt increase my greatness, and comfort me on every side.

16. You have made him the head and not the tail, and he always has the upper hand in every situation. Deut. 28:13 TLB If you will only listen and obey the commandments of the Lord your God that I am giving you today, he will make you the head and not the tail, and you shall always have the upper hand.

17. Thank You, Lord, for giving promotion and power to my pastor. Psalms 75:6 The Book For promotion and power come from nowhere on earth, but only from God.

MY CHURCH

1. You have arisen God, and You have mercy upon our church, for this is Your Your set time to favor us. <u>Psalm 102:13 KJV</u> Thou shalt arise, *and* have mercy upon Zion: for the time to favour her, yea, the set time, is come.

2. In my church we are encouraged in heart and united in love, so that we now have the full riches of complete understanding, so that we are knowing the mystery of God, namely You, Jesus. <u>Col. 2:2 NIV</u> My purpose is that they may be encouraged in heart and united in love, so that they may have the full riches of complete understanding, in order that they may know the mystery of God, namely, Christ.

3. Lord, You have started this good work in my church. You are continuing to help us grow until this task is finally finished. <u>Philip. 1:6 TLB</u> And I am sure that God who began the good work within you will keep right on helping you grow in his grace until his task within you is finally finished on that day when Jesus Christ returns.

4. Lord, You give my church the possession of our land by Your right hand, Your arm and the light of Your Presence, because You favor us. <u>Psalm 44:3 KJV</u> For they got not the land in possession by their own sword, neither did their own arm save them: but thy right hand, and thine arm, and the light of thy countenance, because thou hadst a favour unto them.

5. You justify my Church publicly; You establish its honor and truth before all people. <u>Psalm 7:8 The Book</u> But justify me publicly; establish my honor and truth before them all.

6. Because the people of my Church have show mercy to others and have written Your truth in their hearts, now You and all the people of this city look at us with favor and good understanding. <u>Proverbs 3:3-4 KJV</u> Let not mercy and truth forsake thee: bind them about thy neck; write them upon the table of thine heart: So shalt thou find favour and good understanding in the sight of God and man.

7. Thank You, God, that You have made my Church the head and not the tail. We are above and not beneath, having the upper hand in every situation. <u>Deut. 28:13 KJV</u> And the LORD shall make thee the head, and not the tail; and thou shalt be above only, and thou shalt not be beneath; if that thou hearken to the commandments of the LORD thy God, which I command thee this day, to observe and to do them.

Ruth Shinness 2539 E. 450 N Anderson, IN 46012-9518 Web: www.prayerstrategy.com
e-mail PrayerStrategy@juno.com Phone (765) 643-0612 & (765) 642-0623

MY CHURCH

8. O Lord, You remember my Church with the favor You give to Your people. You visit us with Your salvation. We now share in Your chosen ones' prosperity and rejoice in all their joys, and we receive the glory of Your inheritance that You have for us. Psalm 106:4-5 KJV Remember me, O LORD, with the favour *that thou bearest unto* thy people: O visit me with thy salvation; That I may see the good of thy chosen, that I may rejoice in the gladness of thy nation, that I may glory with thine inheritance.

9. Lord, You are the faithful One who has established this Church and continues to keep it from evil. 2 Thes. 3:3 NKJV But the Lord is faithful, who will establish you and guard you from the evil one.

10. We see the lost of our city repenting and their sins blotted out, and they refresh themselves in Your presence in our Churches. Acts 3:19 KJV Repent ye therefore, and be converted, that your sins may be blotted out, when the times of refreshing shall come from the presence of the Lord.

11. The people of my Church are glad to say, "Let us go to the house of the Lord." Psalm 122:1 KJV I was glad when they said unto me, Let us go into the house of the LORD.

12. You, Lord, make my Church members increase and abound in love one toward another. 1 Thes. 3:12 KJV And the Lord make you to increase and abound in love one toward another, and toward all *men,* even as we *do* toward you.

13. Promotion comes to my Church from You, Lord. You have raised us up. Psalm 75:6 TLB For promotion and power come from nowhere on earth, but only from God. He promotes one and deposes another.

14. The people of my Church speak Your Word with great boldness and You, Lord, stretch forth Your hand to heal and perform miraculous signs and wonders through the name of Jesus. Acts 4:29-30 NIV Now, Lord, consider their threats and enable your servants to speak your word with great boldness. Stretch out your hand to heal and perform miraculous signs and wonders through the name of your holy servant Jesus."

15. You send laborers unto the harvest from my Church. Luke 10:2b KJV Pray ye therefore the Lord of the harvest, that He would send labourers into the harvest.

16. The people in my Church do the good work You have planned for them to do. Ephes. 2:10 KJV For we are his workmanship, created unto Christ Jesus unto good works, which God hath ordained that we should walk in them.

ABIDE

1. I now love You, Lord. You have wanted me to know You and now that has come to pass. Hosea 6:6 TLB I don't want your sacrifices, I want your love, I don't want your offerings--I want you to know me.

2. No matter what happens, I am glad in You, Lord. Philip. 3:1 TLB Whatever happens, dear friends, be glad in the Lord. I never get tired of telling you this, and it is good for you to hear it again and again.

3. Because of my vital need, I have sought, inquired for and required Your presence and now I have that presence with me. Psalms 27:8 AMP You have said Seek my face--inquire for and require my presence [as your vital need]. My heart says to You, Your face [Your presence], Lord, will I seek, and require [of necessity and on the authority of Your Word].

4. Jesus, You love me just like the Father has loved You, and now I continue to live within Your love. John 15:9 TLB "I have loved you even as the Father has loved me. Live within my love."

5. I keep myself in Your love, Lord. Jude 1:21 KJV Keep yourselves in the love of God, looking for the mercy of our Lord Jesus Christ unto eternal life.

6. I am one of the saints in the land; I am one of the glorious ones in whom is all Your delight. Psalm 16:3 NIV As for the saints who are in the land, they are the glorious ones in whom is all my delight.

7. Thank You, Lord, that You have made known to me Your glorious riches, which is You living in me. Col. 1:27 NIV To them God has chosen to make known among the Gentiles the glorious riches of this mystery, which is Christ in you, the hope of glory.

8. My soul finds rest in You alone, God, for You alone are my hope. Psalm 62:5 NIV Find rest, O my soul, in God alone; my hope comes from him.

9. Because I am Your beloved, Lord, I rest securely in You, for You shield me all the day long. I rest between Your shoulders. Deut.33:12 NIV "Let the beloved of the LORD rest secure in him, for he shields him all day long, and the one the LORD loves rests between his shoulders."

10. You have opened up the gates of Your Temple and I go in and give thanks. These gates are the way into Your presence. Psalm 118:19-20 The Book Open the gates of the Temple--I will go in and give him thanks. Those gates are the way into the presence of the Lord, and the godly enter there.

Ruth Shinness 2539 E. 450 N Anderson, IN 46012-9518 Web: www.prayerstrategy.com
e-mail PrayerStrategy@juno.com Phone (765) 643-0612 & (765) 642-0623

ABIDE

11. I have already run for dear life straight into Your arms, God. Psalm 11:1 MES I've already run for dear life straight to the arms of God.

12. I serve You, God and love to praise You. To speak Your name is praise. Just to remember You, God, is a blessing. Psalm 113:1-2 MES You who serve God, praise God! Just to speak his name is praise! Just to remember God is a blessing.

13. I always think of You, Lord, and because You are so near, I never need to stumble or fall. Psalm 16:8 TLB I am always thinking of the Lord; and because he is so near, I never need to stumble or to fall.

14. My heart, body and soul are filled with joy. You are letting me experience the joys of life and the exquisite pleasures of Your own eternal presence. Psalm 16:9, 11 TLB Heart, body, and soul are filled with joy. You have let me experience the joys of life and the exquisite pleasures of your own eternal presence.

15. As long as I live, Lord, I will sing to You. I will praise You to my last breath! I know You are pleased by all my thoughts about You, for You are the source of all my joy. Psalm 104:33-34 TLB I will sing to the Lord as long as I live. I will praise God to my last breath! May he be pleased by all these thoughts about him, for he is the source of all my joy.

16. How precious it is, Lord, to realize that You think about me constantly! I can't even count how many times a day Your thoughts turn toward me. When I waken in the morning, You are still thinking of me! Psalm 139:17-18 TLB Scripture same as above.

17. I am blessed, for You choose me to approach You and dwell in Your courts. I am satisfied with the goodness of Your house, Your holy temple. Psalm 65:4 NKJV Blessed is the man You choose, and cause to approach You, that he may dwell in Your courts. We shall be satisfied with the goodness of Your house, of Your holy temple.

18. I am now Your temple, the home where You live. You live in me, walk with me, and You are my God and I am Your person. 2 Corth. 6:16 TLB You are God's temple, the home of the living God, and God has said of you, "I will live in them and walk among them, and I will be their God and they shall be my people."

19. I now dwell in Your secret place, covered by Your feathers. Under Your wings I always trust. Psalm 91:1,4a TLB He that dwelleth in the secret place of the most high, shall abide under the shadow of the almighty. He shall cover thee with his feathers and under his wings thou shall trust.

Ruth Shinness 2539 E. 450 N. Anderson, IN 46012 Web: www.prayerstrategy.com
e-mail PrayerStrategy@juno.com Phone (765) 643-0612 & (765) 642-0623

15

BENEFITS

1. Thank You, Jesus, that I am Your sheep and I hear Your voice, and You know me and I follow You, and no one is able to snatch me out of Your hand. John 10:27-8 KJV My sheep hear my voice, and I know them, and they follow me. Neither shall any man pluck them out of my hand.

2. Thank You, Lord, that You guide me at all times and satisfy me with all good things. You keep me healthy, and I am like a well-watered garden, like an ever-flowing spring. Isaiah 58:11 AMP And the Lord will guide you continually, and satisfy you with all good things, and keep you healthy too; and you will be like a well-watered garden, like an ever-flowing spring.

3. Thank You that You have preserved me from all evil. Psalm 121:7 KJV The Lord shall preserve thee from all evil: He shall preserve thy soul.

4. You have given me strength and You bless me with peace. Psalm 29:11 KJV The LORD will give strength unto his people: the LORD will bless his people with peace.

5. Thank You that every day You load me with benefits. Psalm 68:19 KJV Blessed be the Lord, who daily loadeth us with benefits, even the God of our salvation.

6. You are the light of my world; I follow You so I don't walk in darkness, but I have Your light of life to lead me. John 8:12 KJV Then spake Jesus again unto them, saying, I am the light of the world: he that followeth me shall not walk in darkness, but shall have the light of life.

7. Lord, I have everything I need for every good work. I not only have enough for my own needs but plenty left over to give joyfully to others. 2 Corth. 9:8 TLB God is able to make it up to you by giving you everything you need and more so that there will not only be enough for your own needs but plenty left over to give joyfully to others.

8. I succeed because You have made me to succeed. Romans 14:4 TEV He shall succeed, because God is able to make him to succeed.

9. You, Christ, have given me the victory in every part of my life, so now wherever I go I tell others about You. I spread this gospel like a sweet perfume. 2 Corth.2:14 TLB But thanks be to God! For through what Christ has done, he has triumphed over us so that now wherever we go he uses us to tell others about the Lord and to spread the Gospel like a sweet perfume.

10. Thank You that blessings now come upon me and overtake me. Deut. 28: 2a KJV And all these blessings shall come on thee, and overtake thee.

Ruth Shinness 2539 E. 450 N Anderson, IN 46012-9518 Web: www.prayerstrategy.com
e-mail PrayerStrategy@juno.com Phone (765) 643-0612 & (765) 642-0623

BENEFITS

11. I do not fear for I have the spirit of power, the spirit of love, and the spirit of a sound mind that You have given me. 2 Timothy 1:7 KJV For God hath not given us the spirit of fear but of power, and of love, and of a sound mind.

12. You have quickened me according to everything that is mine in Your Word. Psalm 119:25b KJV Quicken thou me according to thy Word.

13. Thank You that You have taken all sickness away from the midst of me. Deut. 7:15 KJV And the LORD will take away from thee all sickness.

14. I prosper in everything I put my hand to in the land You have given me. Deut. 28:8 TLB The Lord will bless you with good crops and healthy cattle, and prosper everything you do when you arrive in the land the Lord your God is giving you.

15. Thank You, Lord, for making perfect everything that concerns me. You do not forsake me, for I am the work of Your hands. Psalm 138:8 KJV The LORD will perfect that which concerneth me: thy mercy, O LORD, endureth forever: forsake not the works of thine own hands.

16. Your favor, Lord, is on me and You have established the work of my hands. Psalm 90:17 NIV May the favor of the Lord our God rest upon us; establish the work of our hands for us-- yes, establish the work of our hands.

17. I have risen, I am shining, for You, my light, have come and the glory of Your presence has risen upon me. Isaiah 60:1 NIV Arise, shine; For your light has come! And the glory of the LORD is risen upon you.

18. You are my Lord, You teach me what is best for me and lead me in the way I should go. Isaiah 48:17 NIV This is what the LORD says--your Redeemer, the Holy One of Israel: "I am the LORD your God, who teaches you what is best for you, who directs you in the way you should go.

19. Through You, Christ, I can do all things, for You have strengthened me. Philip. 4:13 KJV I can do all things through Christ which strengtheneth me.

20. Thank You for giving me power to tread on serpents and scorpions and over all the power of the enemy and nothing shall by any means hurt me. Luke 10:19 KJV Behold, I give unto you power to tread on serpents and scorpions and over all the power of the enemy: and nothing shall by any means hurt you.

Ruth Shinness 2539 E. 450 N. Anderson, IN 46012 Web: www.prayerstrategy.com
e-mail PrayerStrategy@juno.com Phone (765) 643-0612 & (765) 642-0623

17

BRINGING UNITY

1. We speak the same thing and there is no division among us, but we are perfectly joined together in the same mind and the same judgment. 1 Corth. 1:10 KJV Now I beseech you, brethren, by the name of our Lord Jesus Christ, that ye all speak the same thing, and that there be no divisions among you; but that ye be perfectly joined together in the same mind and in the same judgment.

2. Thank You, God, You have helped us to live with patience and harmony with each other with Christ-like attitudes, so we praise You with one voice, giving You glory. We now receive each other warmly as Christ received us, so You are glorified. Romans 15:5-7 KJV Now the God of patience and consolation grant you to be like-minded one toward another according to Christ Jesus: That ye may with one mind and one mouth glorify God, even the Father of our Lord Jesus Christ. Wherefore receive ye one another, as Christ also received us to the glory of God.

3. Because we refresh ourselves in Your presence, Lord, we have such joy and fellowship with each other and are able to stay free of sin. 1 John 1:7 TLB But if we are living in the light of God's presence, just as Christ does, then we have wonderful fellowship and joy with each other, and the blood of Jesus his Son cleanses us from every sin.

4. Thank You, Jesus, that You are our way of peace. You have broken down the enemy's wall that separated us. You have made all of us who opposed each other parts of You, and in that way, we have become one. Ephes 2:14 AMP For he himself is our peace - our bond of unity and harmony. He has made us both one (body) and broken down (destroyed, abolished) the hostile dividing wall between us, by abolishing in his own (crucified) flesh the enmity (caused by) the law with its decrees and ordinances - which He annulled: that he from the two might create in Himself one new quality of humanity out of the two - so making peace.

5. We are encouraged in heart and united in love, so that we now have the full riches of complete understanding, so that we know the mystery of God, namely You, Jesus. Col. 2:2 NIV My purpose is that they may be encouraged in heart and united in love, so that they may have the full riches of complete understanding, in order that they may know the mystery of God, namely, Christ.

6. We now keep the unity of the spirit in a bond of peace. Ephes. 4:3 KJV Endeavoring to keep the unity of the Spirit in the bond of peace.

7. We are like one happy family, full of sympathy toward each other, loving one another with tender hearts and humble minds. 1 Peter 3:8 TLB And now this word to all of you: You should be like one big happy family, full of sympathy toward each other, loving one another with tender hearts and humble minds.

Ruth Shinness 2539 E. 450 N Anderson, IN 46012-9518 Web: www.prayerstrategy.com
e-mail PrayerStrategy@juno.com Phone (765) 643-0612 & (765) 642-0623

BRINGING UNITY

8. We are brothers in You, Lord, sharing the same Spirit. Our hearts are tender and sympathetic to each other. We love each other, agreeing wholeheartedly with each other, working together with one heart and mind and purpose. Philip. 2:1b The Book Does it mean anything to you that we are brothers in the Lord sharing the same Spirit? Are your hearts tender and sympathetic at all? Then make me truly happy by loving each other and agreeing wholeheartedly with each other, working together with one heart and mind and purpose.

9. Thank You, Jesus, we are all one as You and the Father are one. People see this, and they believe that You, God, sent Jesus. John 17:21 KJV That they all may be one; as thou, Father, art in me, and I in thee, that they also may be one in us: that the world may believe that thou hast sent me.

10. We have risen and are shining. Our light, which is You, Jesus, has come and Your glory has risen upon us. Isaiah 60:1 KJV Arise, shine; for thy light is come, and the glory of the LORD is risen upon thee.

11. Thank You that You have made our love to grow and overflow to each other and to all men. 1 Thes. 3:12 KJV And the Lord make you to increase and abound in love one toward another, and toward all men, even as we do toward you.

12. It is good and pleasant that we now dwell in unity! Because of our unity, You have commanded a blessing on us, even life forever more. Psalm 133:1,3b KJV Behold, how good and how pleasant it is for brethren to dwell together in unity: for there the LORD commanded the blessing, even life for evermore.

13. I welcome fellow believers who don't see things the way I do, being strong on opinions, but weak in faith. I treat them gently. Romans 14:1 MES Welcome with open arms fellow believers who don't see things the way you do. And don't jump all over them when they do or say something you don't agree with—even when it seems they are strong in opinions and weak in the faith department. Remember they have their own history to deal with. Treat them gently.

14. We believers now agree with one heart and one mind. Acts 4:32a NIV All the believers were one in heart and mind.

15. Lord, You have given us one heart and mind to do Your commandments. 2 Chron. 30:12 KJV In Judah the hand of the Lord was to give them one heart to do the commandments of the king and of the princes, by the word of the Lord.

16. The Glory which God gave You, Jesus, You have given to us, so we are now one, even as You and the Father are one. John 17:22 KJV And the glory which thou gavest me I have given them; that they be made one even as we are one.

Ruth Shinness 2539 E. 450 N. Anderson, IN 46012 Web: www.prayerstrategy.com
e-mail PrayerStrategy@juno.com Phone (765) 643-0612 & (765) 642-0623

19

CHILDREN

1. All of our children are taught of You, Lord, and great is the peace of these children. Isaiah 54:13 KJV And all thy children *shall be* taught of the LORD; and great *shall be* the peace of thy children.

2. You have poured Your Spirit upon our children and Your blessings upon our offspring. They have sprung up as among the grass, as willows by the watercourse. They all proudly say that they belong to You, Lord. Isaiah 44:3-5 TLB I will pour out my Spirit and my blessings on your children. They shall thrive like watered grass, like willows on a riverbank. 'I am the Lord's,' they'll proudly say, or, "I am a Jew," and tattoo upon their hands the name of God or the honored name of Israel.

3. These children have grown and become strong, they are filled with wisdom, and Your grace is upon them. Luke 2:40 NIV And the child grew and became strong; he was filled with wisdom, and the grace of God was upon him.

4. God, You know the thoughts and plans You have for these children; thoughts and plans for their welfare and peace and not for evil, and so we have great hope for their final outcome. Jeremiah 29:11 NIV "For I know the plans I have for you," declares the LORD, "plans to prosper you and not to harm you, plans to give you hope and a future."

5. Thank You, Lord, for sending angels to be with these children, and You are now prospering their way. Genesis 24:40a NKJV But he said to me, 'The LORD, before whom I walk, will send His angel with you and prosper your way.

6. For it is You, God, who is at work within these children, helping them want to obey You, then helping them to do what You want. Philip. 2:13 TLB For God is at work within you, helping you want to obey him, and then helping you do what he wants.

7. The parents have trained their children in the way they should go, and when they are old, they will never leave these teachings. Proverbs 22:6 TLB Teach a child to choose the right path, and when he is older, he will remain upon it.

8. We all fear You and delight in Your commandments, so our children are mighty on the earth; this generation is blessed. Psalm 112:1-2 KJV Blessed *is* the man that feareth the LORD, that delighteth greatly in his commandments. His seed shall be mighty upon earth: the generation of the upright shall be blessed.

9. You order Your angels to protect these children wherever they go. Psalm 91:11 TLB For he orders his angels to protect you wherever you go.

Ruth Shinness 2539 E. 450 N Anderson, IN 46012-9518 Web: www.prayerstrategy.com
e-mail PrayerStrategy@juno.com Phone (765) 643-0612 & (765) 642-0623

CHILDREN

10. Thank You, Lord, that our children are obeying their parents, for this is the right thing to do. They honor their father and mother, so it is going well with them and they are living long in the earth. Ephes. 6:1-3 NIV Children, obey your parents in the Lord, for this is right. "Honor your father and mother"-- which is the first commandment with a promise-- "that it may go well with you and that you may enjoy long life on the earth."

11. You have cleansed our hearts and the hearts of our children to love You, Lord, with all our heart and soul, so we are all alive in You. Deut. 30:6 TLB He will cleanse your hearts and the hearts of your children and of your children's children so that you will love the Lord your God with all your hearts and souls, and Israel shall come alive again!

12. Lord, we thank You that You do not lead our children into temptation, but You have delivered them from evil. Luke 11:4b KJV And lead us not into temptation; but deliver us from evil.

13. Our children have grown in wisdom and stature and favor with You, God, and with man. Luke 2:52 KJV And Jesus increased in wisdom and stature and in favor with God and man.

14. We confess and agree that the parents do not nag or scold these children, making them angry and resentful; rather, they are bringing them up with the loving discipline You approve of, Lord, with suggestions and godly advice. Ephes. 6:4 TLB And now a word to you parents. Don't keep on scolding and nagging your children, making them angry and resentful. Rather, bring them up with the loving discipline the Lord himself approves, with suggestions and godly advice.

15. Lord, You have made our homes strong, blessing our children within. You make peace in our borders and fill us with good healthy food. Psalm 147:13-14 KJV For he hath strengthened the bars of thy gates; he hath blessed thy children within thee. He maketh peace in thy borders, and filleth thee with the finest of the wheat.

16. Thank You, Lord, that You have given our children discretion to preserve them, understanding to keep them, so they are delivered from the way of the evil person who leaves the path of uprightness to walk in the ways of darkness. Proverbs 2:11-14 KJV Discretion shall preserve thee, understanding shall keep thee: To deliver thee from the way of the evil *man,* from the man that speaketh froward things; Who leave the paths of uprightness, to walk in the ways of darkness; Who rejoice to do evil, *and* delight in the frowardness of the wicked.

Ruth Shinness 2539 E. 450 N. Anderson, IN 46012 Web: www.prayerstrategy.com
e-mail PrayerStrategy@juno.com Phone (765) 643-0612 & (765) 642-0623

21

FAMILY

1. People notice that our family belongs to You, Lord, and they stand in awe of us. Deut. 28:10 TLB All the nations in the world shall see that you belong to the Lord, and they will stand in awe.

2. Thank You for giving our family an abundance of good things in the land You have given us. Deut. 28:11 TLB The Lord will give you an abundance of good things in the land, just as he promised: many children, many cattle, and abundant crops.

3. You have blessed the work of our hands. Our families lend and don't have to borrow. Deut. 28:12 TLB He will open to you his wonderful treasury of rain in the heavens, to give you fine crops every season. He will bless everything you do; and you shall lend to many nations, but shall not borrow from them.

4. You have made our family the head and not the tail, always above and never beneath. Deut 28:13 KJV And the LORD shall make thee the head, and not the tail; and thou shalt be above only, and thou shalt not be beneath; if that thou hearken unto the commandments of the LORD thy God, which I command thee this day, to observe and to do them.

5. As for our family, we serve You, Lord, and please You. Joshua 24:15b TLB But as for me and my family, we will serve the Lord.

6. Our family is glad to say, "Let us go to the house of the Lord." Psalm 122:1 KJV I was glad when they said unto me, Let us go into the house of the LORD.

7. You, Lord, have made our family members increase and abound in love one toward another. 1 Thes. 3:12 KJV And the Lord make you to increase and abound in love one toward another, and toward all men, even as we do toward you.

8. Promotion has come from You, Lord. You have raised up our family. Psalm 75:6 TLB For promotion and power come from nowhere on earth, but only from God. He promotes one and deposes another.

9. You have commanded a blessing on our home because our family is dwelling together in unity in such a pleasant way. Psalm 133:1 KJV How good and how pleasant it is for brethern to dwell together in unity.

10. Blessed be You, God and Father of our Lord Jesus Christ, for You have chosen our family from the foundations of the world to bless us with all spiritual blessings in heavenly places in Christ. Ephes. 1:3 KJV Blessed be the God and Father of our Lord Jesus Christ, who hath blessed us with all spiritual blessings in heavenly places in Christ: according as he hath chosen us before the foundation of the world.

Ruth Shinness 2539 E. 450 N Anderson, IN 46012-9518 Web: www.prayerstrategy.com
e-mail PrayerStrategy@juno.com Phone (765) 643-0612 & (765) 642-0623

FAMILY

11. Blessings overtake all of my family because we hearken to Your voice, O Lord. <u>Deut. 28:2 KJV</u> And all these blessings shall come on thee, and overtake thee, if thou shalt hearken unto the voice of the LORD thy God.

12. You are blessing my children, Lord. <u>Deut. 28:4 KJV</u> Blessed *shall be* the fruit of thy body, and the fruit of thy ground, and the fruit of thy cattle, the increase of thy kine, and the flocks of thy sheep.

13. Thank You, Lord, for our family likes being blessed when they come in places and blessed when they go out. <u>Deut. 28:6 KJV</u> Blessed *shalt* thou *be* when thou comest in, and blessed *shalt* thou *be* when thou goest out.

14. Thank You, Lord, that You have defeated all enemies that would come against any in our family. They may come against us in one way, but You scatter them in seven directions. <u>Deut. 28:7 TLB</u> The Lord will defeat your enemies before you; they will march out together against you but scatter before you in seven directions!

15. How blessed we are, Lord, for You have changed our whole family into a holy people, dedicated to You, for we obey You and walk in Your ways. <u>Deut. 28:9 TLB</u> He will change you into a holy people dedicated to himself; this he has promised to do if you will only obey him and walk in his ways.

16. Lord, You have taught our families to declare Your wondrous works. <u>Psalm 71:17 KJV</u> O God, thou hast taught me from my youth: and hitherto have I declared thy wondrous works.

17. O, Lord, because You are working peace and not evil for our families, they have a wonderful future and a great hope. <u>Jeremiah 29:11 NKJV</u> For I know the thoughts I think toward you, says the Lord, thoughts of peace and not of evil, to give you a future and a hope.

18. We know that You, the God of hope, have filled us with all joy and peace in believing, so our families abound in hope, through the power of the Holy Ghost. <u>Romans 15:13 KJV</u> Now the God of hope fill you with all joy and peace in believing, that ye may abound in hope, through the power of the Holy Ghost.

19. In our family, we approve the wonderful things about each other. <u>Philip. 1:10 KJV</u> That ye may approve things that are excellent: that ye may be sincere and without offence till the day of Christ.

Ruth Shinness 2539 E. 450 N. Anderson, IN 46012 Web: www.prayerstrategy.com
e-mail <u>PrayerStrategy@juno.com</u> Phone (765) 643-0612 & (765) 642-0623

23

FAVOR AND HONOR

1. You have risen, God, and now You have mercy upon me, for the time to favor me has come. Psalm 102:13 KJV Thou shalt arise, *and* have mercy upon Zion: for the time to favour her, yea, the set time, is come.

2. Thank You, Lord, I now have favor with everyone who looks upon me. Esther 2:15b KJV Esther obtained favor in the sight of all them that looked upon her.

3. I am no longer called Forsaken and neither is my land called Desolate, for now, Lord, You call me Hephzi-bah, which means You delight in me. You now call my land Beulah, for my land is now married, owned and protected by You, Lord. Thank You that my new name is Sought Out. Isaiah 62:4,12 KJV Thou shalt no more be termed Forsaken; neither shall thy land any more be termed Desolate: but thou shalt be called Hephzi-bah, and thy land Beulah: for the LORD delighteth in thee, and thy land shall be married. And they shall call them, The holy people, The redeemed of the LORD: and thou shalt be called, Sought Out, A city not forsaken.

4. You have called me, Lord, You have blessed me and increased me. You comfort all my waste places and have made my desert like the Garden of Eden. Joy and gladness are now found with me, thanksgiving, and the voice of melody. Isaiah 51:2-3 KJV Look unto Abraham your father, and unto Sarah *that* bare you: for I called him alone, and blessed him, and increased him. For the LORD shall comfort Zion: he will comfort all her waste places; and he will make her wilderness like Eden, and her desert like the garden of the LORD; joy and gladness shall be found therein, thanksgiving, and the voice of melody.

5. Thank You, Lord, that Your favor makes a circle all about me like a shield. Psalm 5:12 KJV For thou, LORD, wilt bless the righteous; with favour wilt thou compass him as *with* a shield.

6. Jesus, we didn't have to fight for our land by our own strength and skill for it is a free gift from You. By Your mighty power You have given it, smiling as You gave it, delighting as You gave it, because You favor us. Psalm 44:3 MES We didn't fight for this land; we didn't work for it—it was a gift! You gave it, smiling as you gave it, delighting as you gave it.

7. I have now found my new life in You, Jesus, so I now have Your favor in everything that concerns my life. Proverbs 8:35 KJV For whoso findeth me findeth life, and shall obtain favour of the LORD.

8. You justify me publicly; You have established my honor and truth before all people. Psalm 7:8 The Book But justify me publicly; establish my honor and truth before them all.

FAVOR AND HONOR

9. Lord, I show mercy to others, and I have written Your truth in my heart, so that now You and all the people look upon me with favor and good understanding. Proverbs 3:3-4 KJV Let not mercy and truth forsake thee: bind them about thy neck; write them upon the table of thine heart: So shalt thou find favour and good understanding in the sight of God and man.

10. Because I tithe, You have opened the windows of heaven and have poured so many blessings on me that I don't have room enough to receive all of them. You have rebuked the devourer over my life, my family and my land. People now call me blessed because You have made me a delightsome land. Malachi 3:10-12 KJV "Bring ye all the tithes into the storehouse, that there may be meat in mine house, and prove me now herewith," saith the LORD of hosts, if I will not open you the windows of heaven, and pour you out a blessing, that there shall not be room enough to receive it and I will rebuke the devourer for your sakes, and he shall not destroy the fruits of your ground; neither shall your vine cast her fruit before the time in the field, saith the LORD of hosts. And all nations shall call you blessed: for ye shall be a delightsome land, saith the LORD of hosts.

11. You think about me, Lord, and visit me, for You have made me a little lower than the angels and have placed a crown of glory and honor upon me. Psalm 8:4-5 KJV What is man, that thou art mindful of him? and the son of man, that thou visitest him? For thou hast made him a little lower than the angels, and hast crowned him with glory and honour.

12. O Lord, You have remembered me with the favor You give to Your people. You have visited me with Your salvation. I now share in Your chosen ones' prosperity and I rejoice in all their joys, and I have received the Glory You have given them. Psalm 106:4-5 NLB Remember me too, O Lord, while you are blessing and saving your people. Let me share in your chosen ones' prosperity and rejoice in all their joys, and receive the glory you give to them.

13. Thank You, God, that You have made me the head and not the tail. I am above only and not beneath, having the upper hand in every situation. Deut. 28:13 KJV And the LORD shall make thee the head, and not the tail; and thou shalt be above only, and thou shalt not be beneath; if that thou hearken unto the commandments of the LORD thy God, which I command thee this day, to observe and to do them.

14. Because You live in me, Christ, I now also receive honor and glory. I am in Your family, God, so that I, too, am a beloved one in whom You are well pleased. 2 Peter 1:17 KJV For he received from God the Father honour and glory, when there came such a voice to him from the excellent glory, This is my beloved Son, in whom I am well pleased.

Ruth Shinness 2539 E. 450 N. Anderson, IN 46012 Web: www.prayerstrategy.com
e-mail PrayerStrategy@juno.com Phone (765) 643-0612 & (765) 642-0623

25

FEAR NOT

1. I sought You Lord, and You heard me, and You delivered me from all my fears. Psalms 34:4 KJV I sought the Lord, and he heard me, and delivered me from all my fears.

2. I am strong and of good courage just as You commanded me to be. I am not afraid or dismayed, for You, Lord, are with me wherever I go. Joshua 1:9 NKJV Have I not commanded you? Be strong and of good courage; do not be afraid, nor be dismayed, for the LORD your God is with you wherever you go."

3. I am not afraid of the battle ahead, for the battle is not mine but Yours, God. I do not need to fight but only to set myself, stand still, and see that Your salvation is with me. 2 Chron. 20:15b,17 NKJV Thus says the LORD to you: "Do not be afraid nor dismayed because of this great multitude, for the battle is not yours, but God's. You will not need to fight in this battle. Position yourselves, stand still and see the salvation of the LORD, who is with you."

4. When I cry to You, Lord, I know You hear me. Then I am able to lie down and sleep in peace and wake up feeling safe, for I know You are watching over me. Psalm 3:4-5 TLB I cried out to the Lord, and he heard me from his Temple in Jerusalem. Then I lay down and slept in peace and woke up safely, for the Lord was watching over me.

5. I know I need not fear, for You, God, are with me; I do not look around in terror nor feel dismayed, for You are my God. You strengthen and harden me to difficulties. Yes, You help me. Yes, You hold me up and retain me with Your victorious right hand of rightness and justice. Isaiah 41:10 AMP Fear not; [there is nothing to fear] for I am with you; do not look around you in terror and be dismayed, for I am your God. I will strengthen and harden you [to difficulties]; yes I will help you; yes, I will hold you up and retain you with My victorious right hand of rightness and justice.

6. Lord, You are the faithful One who has established me and continues to guard me from evil. 2 Thes. 3:3 NKJV But the Lord is faithful, who will establish you and guard you from the evil one.

7. You have said, "I will never leave you nor forsake you." So I boldly say, "Lord, You are my helper, I do not fear. What can man do to me?" Hebrews 13:5b-6 NKJV He Himself has said, "I will never leave you nor forsake you." So we may boldly say: "The LORD is my helper; I will not fear. What can man do to me?"

8. Lord, I fear not, for I shall not be ashamed. Isaiah 54:4 KJV Fear not; for thou shalt not be ashamed.

Ruth Shinness 2539 E. 450 N Anderson, IN 46012-9518 Web: www.prayerstrategy.com
e-mail PrayerStrategy@juno.com Phone (765) 643-0612 & (765) 642-0623

FEAR NOT

9. You are the Lord who created me and who says that I need not be afraid, for You have ransomed me, called me by name and I am Yours. When I go through deep water and trouble, You are with me. When I go through rivers of difficulties, I will not drown! When I walk through the fires of oppression, I will not burn up--the flames will not consume me. You are the Lord my God, my Savior, the Holy One of Israel. Isaiah 43:1-3 TLB But now the Lord who created you, O Israel, says, "Don't be afraid, for I have ransomed you; I have called you by name; you are mine. When you go through deep waters and great trouble, I will be with you. When you go through rivers of difficulty, you will not drown! When you walk through the fire of oppression, you will not be burned up--the flames will not consume you. For I am the Lord your God, your Savior, the Holy One of Israel.

10. Even if ten thousand enemies surround me on every side, I am not afraid. Psalm 3:6 TLB And now, although ten thousand enemies surround me on every side, I am not afraid.

11. Lord, You are my strength, the saving strength for me, Your anointed one. You have saved me and blessed me, for I am Your inheritance: You have fed me and lifted me up forever. Psalm 28:8-9 NIV The LORD is their strength, and he is the saving strength of his anointed. Save thy people, and bless thine inheritance: feed them also, and lift them up for ever.

12. You have given me the authority and power to trample on serpents and scorpions, and physical and mental strength and ability over all the power that the enemy possesses. Nothing shall in any way harm me. Luke 10:19 AMP Behold! I have given you authority and power to trample on serpents and scorpions, and (physical and mental strength and ability) over all the power that the enemy [possesses] and nothing shall in any way harm you.

13. You have saved me to the uttermost for I come to God by You, Jesus, and You live always to intercede for me. Hebrews 7:25 KJV Wherefore he is able also to save them to the uttermost that come unto God by him, seeing he ever liveth to make intercession for them.

14. I shall not fear: for You, Lord, are my God and You fight for me. Deut. 3:22 KJV Ye shall not fear them: for the LORD your God he shall fight for you.

15. I am not afraid when I walk through death's valley, for You are walking by my side. Your shepherd's crook makes me feel secure. Psalm 23:4 MES Even when the way goes through the Death Valley, I'm not afraid when you walk by my side. Your trusty shepherd's crook makes me feel secure.

Ruth Shinness 2539 E. 450 N. Anderson, IN 46012 Web: www.prayerstrategy.com
e-mail PrayerStrategy@juno.com Phone (765) 643-0612 & (765) 642-0623

27

FORGIVING AND BLESSING

1. I have now forgiven anyone who has brought any negative influence into my life and I now set them free for You, God, to work Your best in and through their lives. Mark 11:25 NIV And when you stand praying, if you hold anything against anyone, forgive him, so that your Father in heaven may forgive you your sins.

2. Jesus, I now receive Your forgiveness for any negative influence that has come out of my life to others and I believe You have healed them of emotional hurts they have had because of me. You have also healed the broken places of my heart. Luke 4:18 KJV He hath sent me to heal the brokenhearted.

3. Thank You, Lord, that I have chosen life for myself and my children by choosing to bless others and not to put a curse on them with bad words and thoughts. Deut. 30:19 NIV I call heaven and earth as witnesses today against you, that I have set before you life and death, blessing and cursing; therefore choose life, that both you and your descendants may live.

4. Jesus, I now ask You to bring happiness to any that don't speak kindly to or about me. I now believe You are blessing any that have hurt me. Luke 6:28 TLB Pray for the happiness of those who curse you; implore God's blessing on those who hurt you.

5. Because I have been made a priest unto You, Lord, I am praying this prayer over my family, others, and even my enemies, that You bless and protect them. Your face radiates with joy because of them. You are gracious to them, showing them favor, and You have given them Your peace. You are now personally blessing them. Numbers 6:22-27 TLB Now the Lord said to Moses, "Tell Aaron and his sons that they are to give this special blessing to the people of Israel: 'May the Lord bless and protect you; may the Lord's face radiate with joy because of you; may he be gracious to you, show you his favor, and give you his peace.' This is how Aaron and his sons shall call down my blessings upon the people of Israel; and I myself will personally bless them." Rev. 1:6 TLB He has gathered us into his Kingdom and made us priests of God his Father.

6. I confess my sin of unforgiveness, and You forgive me and have cleansed me from this unrighteousness. 1 John1:9 KJV If we confess our sins, he is faithful and just to forgive us our sins, and to cleans us from all unrighteousness.

7. I now have the grace to remain calm, take second place and forgive quickly as You my Master have forgiven me. Col. 3:13 the MES Be even-tempered, content with second place, quick to forgive an offense. Forgive as quickly and completely as the Master forgave you.

Ruth Shinness 2539 E. 450 N Anderson, IN 46012-9518 Web: www.prayerstrategy.com
e-mail PrayerStrategy@juno.com Phone (765) 643-0612 & (765) 642-0623

FORGIVING AND BLESSING

8. Thank You, Jesus, that we are like one happy family, for we are full of sympathy toward one another. We love one another with tender hearts. We don't mind taking second place, for we have humble minds. 1 Peter 3:8 TLB And now this word to all of you: You should be like one big happy family, full of sympathy toward each other, loving one another with tender hearts and humble minds.

9. Thank You, Lord, that when someone does evil to me, I don't pay back with evil. Instead of snapping back with unkind words, I pray that You will help them. For in being kind to others, You are continually blessing me. 1 Peter 3:9 TLB Don't repay evil for evil. Don't snap back at those who say unkind things about you. Instead, pray for God's help for them, for we are to be kind to others, and God will bless us for it.

10. I now know more and have greater discernment on how to have my love abound toward others. Instead of looking at the bad, I am now able to approve what is excellent, so I am sincere and without offense until the day of Christ. I am filled with the good fruits of righteousness that You have given me, Christ, which is all to Your glory. Philip.1:9-11 KJV And this I pray, that your love may abound still more and more in knowledge and all Judgement, that you may approve the things that are excellent, that you may be sincere and without offense till the day of Christ, being filled with the fruits of righteousness which are by Jesus Christ, to the glory and praise of God.

11. I now love my enemies, Lord. I have chosen to bless any that curse me. I am thinking of good things to do to people who hate me. I am praying for people who despitefully use me and persecute me. Matthew 5:44 KJV But I say unto you, Love your enemies, bless them that curse you, do good to them that hate you, and pray for them which despitefully use you, and persecute you.

12. Lord, when I criticize and condemn others, I have noticed that it comes back on me. Ouch! I have learned my lesson, I now go easy on others. I am now so much happier. Luke 6:37 The Book Never criticize or condemn or it will come back on you. Go easy on others; then they will do the same for you.

13. Because I now walk in the light of Your presence, I have good fellowship with others, for Your blood has cleansed me from all sin. 1 John 1:7 KJV But if we walk in the light as he is in the light, we have fellowship one with another, and the blood of Jesus Christ his Son cleanseth us from all sin.

14. For my enemies, I pray that You are now working Your good in and through their lives. Matt. 5:44 The Book But I say: Love your enemies! Pray for those who persecute you!

FOR OUR PEOPLE

Blessings are now overtaking me for I listen to Your voice, Lord, so I am blessed wherever I am. My children and even my animals are blessed by You. My grocery sacks are full and so are my cupboards. I am blessed when I come in and blessed when I go out. If enemies rise against me, they are defeated before my face and flee from me. Everything I set my hand to is blessed. I am blessed in the land You have given me. You have established me as a holy person unto Yourself because I keep Your commandments and walk in Your ways. All the people see that I belong to You and they are afraid of me. I prosper in every way. Whatever I put my hand to do is blessed. I lend but do not have to borrow. Thank You for making me the head and not the tail and above only and not beneath, all because I do what You command.

Abraham's blessing through what Jesus did for us.

Galatians 3:13,14 TLB   But Christ has brought us out from under the doom of that impossible system by taking the curse for our wrongdoing upon himself. For it is written in the Scripture, "Anyone who is hanged on a tree is cursed" [as Jesus was hung upon a wooden cross]. Now God can bless the Gentiles, too, with this same blessing he promised to Abraham; and all of us as Christians can have the promised Holy Spirit through this faith.

Abraham's Blessings

Deut. 28:2-13 KJV   And all these blessings shall come on thee, and overtake thee, if thou shalt hearken unto the voice of the LORD thy God. [3] Blessed shalt thou be in the city, and blessed shalt thou be in the field. [4] Blessed shall be the fruit of thy body, and the fruit of thy ground, and the fruit of thy cattle, the increase of thy kine, and the flocks of thy sheep. [5] Blessed shall be thy basket and thy store. [6] Blessed shalt thou be when thou comest in, and blessed shalt thou be when thou goest out. [7] The LORD shall cause thine enemies that rise up against thee to be smitten before thy face: they shall come out against thee one way, and flee before thee seven ways. [8] The LORD shall command the blessing upon thee in thy storehouses, and in all that thou settest thine hand unto; and he shall bless thee in the land which the LORD thy God giveth thee. [9] The LORD shall establish thee an holy people unto himself, as he hath sworn unto thee, if thou shalt keep the commandments of the LORD thy God, and walk in his ways. [10] And all people of the earth shall see that thou art called by the name of the LORD; and they shall be afraid of thee. [11] And the LORD shall make thee plenteous in goods, in the fruit of thy body, and in the fruit of thy cattle, and in the fruit of thy ground, in the land which the LORD sware unto thy fathers to give thee. [12] The LORD shall open unto thee his good treasure, the heaven to give the rain unto thy land in his season, and to bless all the work of thine hand: and thou shalt lend unto many nations, and thou shalt not borrow. [13] And the LORD shall make thee the head, and not the tail; and thou shalt be above only, and thou shalt not be beneath; if that thou hearken unto the commandments of the LORD thy God, which I command thee this day, to observe and to do them.

Ruth Shinness 2539 E. 450 N Anderson, IN 46012-9518 Web: www.prayerstrategy.com
e-mail PrayerStrategy@juno.com Phone (765) 643-0612 & (765) 642-0623

FOR OUR PEOPLE

1. Thank You, Lord, that You have given me the gift of enjoying the good of all the work I do. Eccles. 3:13 KJV And also that every man should eat and drink, and enjoy the good of all his labour, it is a gift of God.

2. I work with all my might and I do it all in Your name, giving thanks to You. Eccles. 9:10a KJV Whatsoever thy hand findeth to do, do it with thy might.

3. Your beauty, Lord, is upon me, and You have established the work of my hands. Psalm 90:17 KJV And let the beauty of the LORD our God be upon us: and establish thou the work of our hands upon us; yea, the work of our hands establish thou it.

4. Thank You that I live a quiet life, minding my own business and doing my own work, so people who are not Christians trust and respect me and I do not need to depend on others for enough money to pay my bills. 1Thes. 4:11-12 TLB This should be your ambition: to live a quiet life, minding your own business and doing your own work, just as we told you before. As a result, people who are not Christians will trust and respect you, and you will not need to depend on others for enough money to pay your bills.

5. I am glad, Lord, that all my debts are paid, except the debt of loving others, which I can never finish paying. I obey You by loving others, which fills all Your requirements. Romans 13:8 TLB Pay all your debts except the debt of love for others--never finish paying that! For if you love them, you will be obeying all of God's laws, fulfilling all his requirements.

6. Lord, I am doing a good work and I am not discouraged, for You are rewarding me. 2 Chron. 15:7 TLB You men of Judah, keep up the good work and don't get discouraged, for you will be rewarded."

7. In everything I do, I have great success, for You, Lord, are with me. 1 Sam. 18:14 NIV In everything he did he had great success, because the LORD was with him.

8. Those around me shout for joy and are glad, and favor Your righteous cause and say over and over, "Let the Lord be magnified," for You have pleasure in my prosperity. Psalm 35:27 KJV Let them shout for joy, and be glad, that favour my righteous cause: yea, let them say continually, Let the LORD be magnified, which hath pleasure in the prosperity of his servant.

9. Thank You, Jesus, for supplying all my needs out of Your riches in glory by Christ Jesus. Philip. 4:19 KJV But my God shall supply all your need according to his riches in glory by Christ Jesus.

Ruth Shinness 2539 E. 450 N. Anderson, IN 46012   Web: www.prayerstrategy.com
e-mail PrayerStrategy@juno.com Phone (765) 643-0612 & (765) 642-0623

31

GOD'S LOVE TO ME

1. I believe that my heart is now flooded with light so I am seeing something of the future I have been called to share with You, Christ. Ephes.1:18a TLB   I pray that your hearts will be flooded with light so that you can see something of the future he has called you to share.

2. You have been made rich, God, because I, who belong to Christ, have been given to You. Ephes. 1:18b TLB   I want you to realize that God has been made rich because we who are Christ's have been given to him!

3. I am understanding how great Your power is to help a believer like me. This power that helps me is the same power that raised You from the dead. I am now a part of Your church, Christ, filled up with You. Ephes. 1:19 TLB   I pray that you will begin to understand how incredibly great his power is to help those who believe him. It is that same mighty power that raised Christ from the dead and seated him in the place of honor at God's right hand in heaven, far, far above any other king or ruler or dictator or leader. Yes, his honor is far more glorious than that of anyone else either in this world or in the world to come. And God has put all things under his feet and made him the supreme Head of the Church - which is his body, filled with himself, the Author and Giver of everything everywhere.

4. Because You are in me, Christ, I am a new creation; the old has gone and the new has come. These new things are of You, God. You have reconciled me to Yourself through Christ and have given me a ministry of reconciling others to You. 2 Corth. 5:17-19 NIV   Therefore, if anyone is in Christ, he is a new creation; the old has gone, the new has come! All this is from God, who reconciled us to himself through Christ and gave us the ministry of reconciliation: that God was reconciling the world to himself in Christ, not counting men's sins against them. And he has committed to us the message of reconciliation.

5. Lord, You have come to live with me. You are my mighty savior. You have given me the victory. You rejoice over me with gladness; You love me and don't accuse me. Zeph. 3:17 TLB   But the Lord your God has arrived to live among you, He is a mighty savior. He will give you the victory. He will rejoice over you with great gladness; he will love you and not accuse you.

6. Lord, is that a joyous choir I hear? No, it is You Yourself exulting over me with a happy song. Zeph. 3:18 TLB   "Is that a joyous choir I hear?" No, it is the Lord himself exulting over you in happy song.

7. Because I have the spirit which is of You, God, I am knowing the things that You have freely given me. 1 Corth 2:12 KJV   Now we have received, not the spirit of the world, but the spirit which is of God; that we might know the things that are freely given to us of God.

GOD'S LOVE TO ME

8. Thank You, Lord, You have blessed me with every blessing in heaven because I belong to You. <u>Ephes. 1:3 TLB</u> How we praise God, the Father of our Lord Jesus Christ, who has blessed us with every blessing in heaven because we belong to Christ.

9. Before the world was made, God, You chose me to be Yours by what Christ would do for me. You have made me holy in Your eyes, without a single fault. I now stand before You, God, covered by Your love. <u>Ephes. 1:4 TLB</u> Long ago, even before he made the world, God chose us to be his very own through what Christ would do for us; he decided then to make us holy in his eyes, without a single fault--we who stand before him covered with his love.

10. God, Your plan has always been to adopt me into Your own family by sending Jesus Christ to die for me. You did this for me because You wanted to. <u>Ephes. 1:5 TLB</u> His unchanging plan has always been to adopt us into his own family by sending Jesus Christ to die for us. And he did this because he wanted to!

11. Praise You, God, for this wonderful kindness and favor You have poured out on me, because I belong to Your dearly loved Son. <u>Ephes. 1:6 TLB</u> Now all praise to God for his wonderful kindness to us and his favor that he has poured out upon us because we belong to his dearly loved Son.

12. God, Your kindness is so overwhelming for taking away all of my sins by the blood of Your Son, by whom I am saved. <u>Ephes. 1:7 TLB</u> So overflowing is his kindness toward us that he took away all our sins through the blood of his Son, by whom we are saved.

13. You have showered Your rich grace upon me, for You understand me and know what is best for me at all times. <u>Ephes. 1:8 TLB</u> And he has showered down upon us the richness of his grace--for how well he understands us and knows what is best for us at all times.

14. I believe that because of prayer, You, God, have answered and have given me wisdom to see clearly who Christ is and all He has done for me. <u>Ephes. 1:16-17 TLB</u> I have never stopped thanking God for you. I pray for you constantly, asking God, the glorious Father of our Lord Jesus Christ, to give you wisdom to see clearly and really understand who Christ is and all that he has done for you.

15. I am now walking in Your fullness of life and I know that is Your purpose for me. <u>John 10:10 The Book</u> The thief's purpose is to steal, kill, and destroy. My purpose is to give life in all its fullness.

16. Suddenly, God, You floodlight my life; I blaze with glory, Your glory! <u>Psalm 18:28 MES</u> Suddenly, GOD, you floodlight my life; I'm blazing with glory, Your glory!

Ruth Shinness 2539 E. 450 N. Anderson, IN 46012 Web: www.prayerstrategy.com
e-mail PrayerStrategy@juno.com Phone (765) 643-0612 & (765) 642-0623

33

GO YE

1. Just as the Father has sent You Jesus, so now You have sent me. John 20:21 NKJV So Jesus said to them again, "Peace to you! As the Father has sent Me, I also send you."

2. Thank You that I have received power, for the Holy Ghost has come upon me. I am a witness to my own region, to Jerusalem, Judea, Samaria and to the uttermost parts of the earth. Acts 1:8 KJV But ye shall receive power, after that the Holy Ghost is come upon you: and ye shall be witnesses unto me both in Jerusalem, and in all Judea, and in Samaria, and unto the uttermost part of the earth.

3. I am going forth and preaching everywhere and You, Lord, are working with me, confirming the Word with signs following. Mark 16:20 KJV And they went forth, and preached every where, the Lord working with them, and confirming the word with signs following. Amen.

4. You have chosen and ordained me, Jesus, so that I go out and bring forth fruit. John 15:16 KJV Ye have not chosen me, but I have chosen you, and ordained you, that ye should go and bring forth fruit, and that your fruit should remain: that whatsoever ye shall ask of the Father in my name, he may give it you.

5. Since I am Christ's ambassador, God, You are making Your appeal through me. I am begging people for Your sake to lay hold of this divine favor and be reconciled to You. 2 Cor. 5:20 NKJV Now then, we are ambassadors for Christ, as though God were pleading through us: we implore you on Christ's behalf, be reconciled to God.

6. Because I follow after You, Jesus, You have made me to become a fisher of men. Mark 1:17 KJV And Jesus said unto them, Come ye after me, and I will make you to become fishers of men.

7. Jesus, You have given me utterance and I open my mouth boldly and make known the mystery of the gospel and I speak boldly as I ought. Ephes. 6:19-20 NKJV And for me, that utterance may be given to me, that I may open my mouth boldly to make known the mystery of the gospel, for which I am an ambassador in chains; that in it I may speak boldly, as I ought to speak.

8. Lord, I tell everyone the good news that You forgive people's sins. I have not been too shy to do this. I do not keep this good news hidden in my heart, but proclaim everywhere Your loving kindness and truth. Psalm 40:9 The Book I have told everyone the good news that you forgive people's sins. I have not been timid about it as You know, O Lord. I have not kept this good news hidden in my heart, but have proclaimed Your lovingkindness and truth to all the congregation.

Ruth Shinness 2539 E. 450 N Anderson, IN 46012-9518 Web: www.prayerstrategy.com
e-mail PrayerStrategy@juno.com Phone (765) 643-0612 & (765) 642-0623

GO YE

9. I believe in You, Jesus, so that the works You did, I do also; and I do even greater works, because You have gone to the Father. John 14:12 KJV Verily, verily, I say unto you, He that believeth on me, the works that I do shall he do also; and greater works than these shall he do; because I go unto my Father.

10. Because of John 14:12, (above): Your Spirit, Lord is upon me and I am anointed to preach the gospel to the poor; I am sent to heal the brokenhearted, to preach deliverance to the captives, to recover the sight to the blind, and to set at liberty them that are bruised. Luke 4:18 KJV The Spirit of the Lord is upon me, because he hath anointed me to preach the gospel to the poor; he hath sent me to heal the brokenhearted, to preach deliverance to the captives, and recovering of sight to the blind, to set at liberty them that are bruised.

11. Thank You that I am now doing the good work that You have planned for me to do. Ephes. 2:10 KJV For we are his workmanship, created in Christ Jesus unto good works, which God hath before ordained that we should walk in them.

12. I am going around the world with news of Your salvation and Your plan for all people. Psalm 67:2 TLB Send us around the world with the news of your saving power and your eternal plan for all mankind.

13. In You, Jesus, in every respect, I am enriched in full power and readiness to speak of my faith. I have complete knowledge and illumination that gives me full insight into its meaning. 1 Corth. 1:5 AMP In Him in every respect you were enriched, in full power and readiness of speech [to speak of your faith] and complete knowledge and illumination [to give you full insight into its meaning.

14. Thank You, God, for bringing me to You through what Christ has done. You have given me the privilege of urging everyone to come into Your favor and be reconciled to You. 2 Corth. 5:18 TLB All these new things are from God who brought us back to himself through what Christ Jesus did. And God has given us the privilege of urging everyone to come into his favor and be reconciled to him.

15. I have heard Your voice say, "Who shall I send, and who will go for Me?" I say to You, Lord, "Now You have sent me." Isaiah 6:8 KJV Also I heard the voice of the Lord, saying, Whom shall I send, and who will go for us? Then said I, Here am I; send me.

16. Thank You, God, You always cause me to triumph wherever I go, as You manifest the sweetness of Your knowledge through me as I speak. 2 Corth. 2:14 KJV Now thanks be unto God, which always causeth us to triumph in Christ, and maketh manifest the savor of his knowledge by us in everyplace.

Ruth Shinness 2539 E. 450 N. Anderson, IN 46012 Web: www.prayerstrategy.com
e-mail PrayerStrategy@juno.com Phone (765) 643-0612 & (765) 642-0623

35

GO YE

17. Thank You, Lord, for helping me tell others about Your agreement to save people. I don't tell them that they must obey the law or die, but that there is life for them in the Holy Spirit. 2 Corth. 3:6 TLB He is the one who has helped us tell others about his new agreement to save them. We do not tell them that they must obey every law of God or die; but we tell them there is life for them from the Holy Spirit. The old way, trying to be saved by keeping the Ten Commandments, ends in death; in the new way, the Holy Spirit gives them life.

18. I am called in righteousness, and You hold my hand and keep me. I am a light to others, to open blind eyes, and to bring prisoners out of their prison house of darkness. Isaiah 42:6-7 KJV I the LORD have called thee in righteousness, and will hold thine hand, and will keep thee, and give thee for a covenant of the people, for a light of the Gentiles; To open the blind eyes, to bring out the prisoners from the prison, and them that sit in darkness out of the prison house.

19. I heal the sick and say, "The Kingdom of God is near you." Luke 10:9 TLB Heal the sick; and as you heal them, say, 'The Kingdom of God is very near you now.'

20. Through You, Jesus, I have received my apostleship to promote obedience to the faith and make disciples for Your name's sake among all the nations. Romans 1:5-6 AMP It is through Him that we have received grace (God's unmerited favor) and [our] apostleship to promote obedience to the faith and make disciples for His name's sake among all the nations, and this includes you, called of Jesus Christ and invited [as you are] to belong to Him.

21. Though I don't deserve it, Lord, You have chosen me for this special joy of telling everyone the good news of the endless treasures available to them, for You live in me. Ephes. 3:8 TLB Just think! Though I did nothing to deserve it, and though I am the most useless Christian there is, yet I was the one chosen for this special joy of telling the Gentiles the Glad News of the endless treasures available to them in Christ.

22. I believe on You, Jesus, so rivers of living water flow out of me. John 7:38 KJV He that believeth on me, out of his belly shall flow rivers of living water.

23. You have given me the heathen for my inheritance and I now go to the uttermost parts of the earth and possess nations. Psalm 2:8 KJV Ask of me, and I shall give thee the heathen for thine inheritance, and the uttermost parts of the earth for thy possession.

24. I have prayed for You to send laborers into the harvest, now You have sent them and me also. Luke 10:2b KJV Pray ye therefore the Lord of the harvest, that he would send forth labourers into the harvest.

Ruth Shinness 2539 E. 450 N Anderson, IN 46012-9518 Web: www.prayerstrategy.com
e-mail PrayerStrategy@juno.com Phone (765) 643-0612 & (765) 642-0623

GO YE

25. I am speaking Your Word with great boldness; and You, Lord, have stretched forth Your hand to heal and have performed miraculous signs and wonders through the name of Jesus. Acts 4:29-30 NIV Now, Lord, consider their threats and enable your servants to speak your word with great boldness. Stretch out your hand to heal and perform miraculous signs and wonders through the name of your holy servant Jesus."

26. I am called Your priest, Lord, a minister of our God. I am fed with the treasures of the nations and am glorying in their riches. Isaiah 61:6 TLB You shall be called priests of the Lord, ministers of our God. You shall be fed with the treasures of the nations and shall glory in their riches.

27. There is a sweet fragrance of You, Christ, within me, an aroma to both the saved and the unsaved all around me everywhere I go. 2 Corth. 2:15 TLB As far as God is concerned there is a sweet, wholesome fragrance in our lives. It is the fragrance of Christ within us, an aroma to both the saved and the unsaved all around us.

28. I am now preaching the Word, being instant in season and out, reproving, rebuking, exhorting with long suffering and doctrine. 2 Timothy 4:1-2 KJV I charge thee therefore before God, and the Lord Jesus Christ, who shall judge the quick and the dead at his appearing and his kingdom; Preach the word; be instant in season, out of season; reprove, rebuke, exhort with all longsuffering and doctrine.

29. In Your name, Jesus, I cast out demons, speak in new tongues, take up serpents, and am not hurt by drinking deadly things. I lay hands on the sick and they recover. You are working with me, confirming the Word with signs following. Mark 16:17,18,20 NKJV And these signs will follow those who believe: In My name they will cast out demons; they will speak with new tongues; they will take up serpents; and if they drink anything deadly, it will by no means hurt them; they will lay hands on the sick, and they will recover. And they went out and preached everywhere, the Lord working with them and confirming the word through the accompanying signs. Amen.

30. Lord, Your Word says my feet are beautiful, for You send me to preach the gospel of peace and to bring glad tidings of good things. Romans 10:15 KJV And how shall they preach, except they be sent? as it is written, How beautiful are the feet of them that preach the gospel of peace, and bring glad tidings of good things!

31. Lord, You have given me a new song to sing. Now many hear the glorious things You have done for me; they are in awe and put their trust in You. Psalm 40:3 The Book He has given me a new song to sing, of praises to our God. Now many will hear of the glorious things he did for me, and stand in awe before the Lord, and put their trust in him.

Ruth Shinness 2539 E. 450 N. Anderson, IN 46012 Web: www.prayerstrategy.com
e-mail PrayerStrategy@juno.com Phone (765) 643-0612 & (765) 642-0623

37

GUIDANCE

1. You are my shepherd. I am resting in green pastures, by the quiet waters. You have restored my soul, and I now walk in the right path You have planned for me. Psalm 23: 1-3 KJV The Lord is my shepherd; I shall not want. He maketh me to lie down in green pastures: He leadeth me beside the still waters. He restoreth my soul; He leadeth me in the paths of righteousness for his namesake.

2. Thank You, Jesus, that I am Your sheep and I hear Your voice, You know me and I follow You, and no one is able to snatch me out of Your hand. John 10:27 KJV My sheep hear my voice, and I know them, and they follow me.

3. Thank You, Lord, that You guide me at all the times and satisfy me with all kinds of good things. I am healthy like an ever-flowing spring of water. Isaiah 58:11 KJV And the Lord will guide you continually, and satisfy thy soul in drought, and make fat thy bones: and thou shall be like a watered garden, and like a spring of water, whose waters fail not.

4. You are my Lord; You teach me what is best for me and lead me in the way I should go. Isaiah 48:17 NIV This is what the LORD says--your Redeemer, the Holy One of Israel: "I am the LORD your God, who teaches you what is best for you, who directs you in the way you should go."

5. Lord, my ears hear Your Word telling me, "This is the way, walk in it, when you turn to the right hand and when you turn to the left." Isaiah 30:21 KJV And thy ears shall hear a word behind thee, saying, "This is the way, walk thee in it, when ye turn to the right hand and when ye turn to the left."

6. Blessings overtake me because I pay attention to Your voice, O Lord. Deut. 28:2 KJV And all these blessings shall come on thee, and overtake thee, if thou shalt hearken unto the voice of the LORD thy God.

7. My heart is flooded with light, so I know something of the future You have called me to share with You. I now understand how great Your power is to help a believer like me. Ephes. 1:18-19 TLB I pray that your hearts will be flooded with light so that you can see something of the future he has called you to share. I want you to realize that God has been made rich because we who are Christ's have been given to him! I pray that you will begin to understand how incredibly great his great power to help those who believe him.

8. I confess that You are now leading me by Your Spirit this very day. Romans 8:14 KJV As many as are led by the Spirit of God, they are the sons of God.

9. The Spirit of truth has come and is guiding me into all truth. John 16:13a NIV But when he, the Spirit of truth, comes, he will guide you into all truth.

Ruth Shinness 2539 E. 450 N Anderson, IN 46012-9518 Web: www.prayerstrategy.com
e-mail PrayerStrategy@juno.com Phone (765) 643-0612 & (765) 642-0623

GUIDANCE

10. Lord, thank You for making my path brighter and easier to follow each day. Proverbs 4:18 KJV The path of the just is as a shining light, that shineth more and more unto the perfect day.

11. I am trusting You, Lord, with all my heart, and do not try to figure out everything with my own understanding. I give You credit in all I do, so You are now directing my paths. Proverbs 3:5-6 KJV Trust in the Lord with all thine heart; lean not unto thine own understanding. In all thy ways acknowledge him and he shall direct thy paths.

12. I make my plans, but You, God, direct my steps. Proverbs 16:9 KJV A man's heart deviseth his way; but the Lord directeth his steps.

13. You cause me to hear Your lovingkindness in the morning, for I trust in You. You cause me to know the way I should walk, for I lift up my soul unto You. Psalm 143:8 KJV Cause me to hear thy lovingkindness in the morning; for in thee do I trust: cause me to know the way wherein I should walk: for I lift up my soul unto thee.

14. You have shown me the path of life and I now live in Your presence, full of Your joy. At Your right hand, I am experiencing Your pleasures forevermore. Psalm 16:11 KJV Thou wilt show me the path of life: in thy presence is fullness of joy; at thy right hand there are pleasures forevermore.

15. You are the light of my world and I follow You so I don't walk in darkness. Your light of life shines in me. John 8:12 KJV Then spake Jesus unto them saying, "I am the light of the world: he that followeth me shall not walk in darkness, but shall have the light of life."

16. You instruct me and teach me in the way I should go. You guide me with Your eye. I am not like the horse or mule that needs a bit and bridle in my mouth to be led in the right way. Psalm 32:8-9 KJV I will instruct thee and teach thee in the way thou should go: I will guide thee with mine eye. Be ye not as the horse, or as the mule, which have no understanding: whose mouth must be held in with bit and bridle, lest they come near unto thee.

17. My steps are ordered by You, Lord, and You delight in all my ways. Psalm 37:23 KJV The steps of a good man are ordered by the Lord: and he delighteth in all his ways.

18. You have given light to me in my darkness. You are guiding my feet in the way of peace. Luke 1:79 KJV To give light to them that sit in darkness and in the shadow of death, to guide our feet into the way of peace.

Ruth Shinness 2539 E. 450 N. Anderson, IN 46012 Web: www.prayerstrategy.com
e-mail PrayerStrategy@juno.com Phone (765) 643-0612 & (765) 642-0623

39

HEALING

1. Thank You, Lord, You have brought health to me and have cured me and now You have revealed to me an abundance of peace and truth. Jeremiah 33:6 Behold, I will bring it health and cure, and I will cure them, and will reveal unto them the abundance of peace and truth.

2. You also have given me power against all unclean spirits, to cast them out, and to heal all manner of sickness and all diseases. Matthew 10:1 KJV And when he had called unto *him* his twelve disciples, he gave them power *against* unclean spirits, to cast them out, and to heal all manner of sickness and all manner of disease.

3. Thank You, Jesus, You have already risen with healing in Your wings and I am free, leaping with joy like a calf let out to pasture. Malachi 4:2 TLB "But for you who fear my name, the Son of Righteousness will rise with healing in his wings. And you will go free, leaping with joy like calves let out to pasture.

4. Jesus, You were wounded and bruised for my sins; You were beaten, so now I can have peace and because You were lashed, I am now healed. Isaiah 53:5 TLB But he was wounded and bruised for our sins. He was beaten that we might have peace; he was lashed--and we were healed! 1 Peter 2:24 TLB He personally carried the load of our sins in his own body when he died on the cross so that we can be finished with sin and live a good life from now on. For his wounds have healed ours!

5. I bless You with all my soul, Lord, for You said not to forget Your benefits. Thank You for forgiving all of my sins and healing all of my diseases. Psalm 103:2-3 NIV Praise the LORD, O my soul, and forget not all his benefits-- who forgives all your sins and heals all your diseases.

6. The Holy Spirit who raised You from the dead, Jesus, is living in me and has given life to my body through Your Spirit that lives in me. Romans 8:11 NIV And if the Spirit of him who raised Jesus from the dead is living in you, he who raised Christ from the dead will also give life to your mortal bodies through his Spirit, who lives in you.

7. I rejoice, for Your Word has healed me and delivered me from destruction. Psalm 107:20 KJV He sent his word, and healed them, and delivered them from their destruction.

8. By Your right hand, Lord, You do great things, for I shall not die but live to declare Your wonderful works. Psalm 118:16-17 KJV The right hand of the LORD is exalted: the right hand of the LORD doeth valiantly. I shall not die, but live, and declare the works of the LORD.

Ruth Shinness 2539 E. 450 N Anderson, IN 46012-9518 Web: www.prayerstrategy.com
e-mail PrayerStrategy@juno.com Phone (765) 643-0612 & (765) 642-0623

HEALING

9. Jesus, You took my infirmities, so I don't have them. You carried away my diseases, so they are far from me. I know that Your life is now flowing through me and You have brought healing to every cell of my being. Matthew 8:17 NKJV That it might be fulfilled which was spoken by Isaiah the prophet, saying: "He Himself took our infirmities and bore our sicknesses." John 6:63 KJV It is the spirit that quickeneth; the flesh profiteth nothing: the words that I speak unto you, they are spirit, and they are life.

10. Thank You, Lord, for keeping evil and plagues away from me and my home. Psalms 91:10 NKJV No evil shall befall you, nor shall any plague come near your dwelling.

11. We are confessing our sins to one another and praying for each other, so now we can live together whole and healed. James 5:16 MES Make this your common practice: Confess your sins to each other and pray for each other so that you can live together whole and healed.

12. I listen to Your Words carefully. I am keeping these thoughts always in my mind so they penetrate deep in my heart, for they mean real life to me and health to all my flesh. Proverbs 4:20-22 TLB Listen, son of mine, to what I say. Listen carefully. Keep these thoughts ever in mind; let them penetrate deep within your heart, for they will mean real life for you and radiant health.

13. You accept me like You did Abraham because I trust You when Your Word says I am healed. Even when I don't feel like I am healed, I say I am healed, for You, God, call those things that be not as though they were. Romans 4:17 TLB God will accept all people in every nation who trust God as Abraham did. And this promise is from God himself, who makes the dead live again and speaks of future events with as much certainty as though they were already past. 1 Peter 2:24b KJV By whose stripes ye were healed.

14. I have asked for healing, so I believe I have received it and the healing is now mine. Mark 11:24 KJV Therefore I tell you, whatever you ask for in prayer, believe that you have received it and it will be yours.

15. I am enjoying good health and all is going well with me, even as my soul is getting along well. 3 John 2 NIV I pray that you may enjoy good health and that all may go well with you, even as your soul is getting along well.

16. Thank You, Lord, You have taken away all my sickness, and You do not let me suffer the sickness of other peoples. Deut. 8:15 TLB The Lord will take away all your sickness and will not let you suffer any of the diseases of Egypt you remember so well; he will give them all to your enemies.

HEALTHY AGING

1. You are my God through all my lifetime, yes, even when my hair is white with age. You made me and You are taking care of me. You carry me along and are my Savior. Isaiah 46:4 TLB I will be your God through all your lifetime, yes, even when your hair is white with age. I made you and I will care for you. I will carry you along and be your Savior.

2. I serve You, Lord, and You have blessed my bread and my water and You have taken sickness away from the inside of me. Exodus 23:25 KJV And ye shall serve the Lord your God, and he shall bless thy bread, and thy water: and I will take sickness away from the midst of thee.

3. Thank You for I have Your Wisdom working in me, God, to give me a long good life, riches, honor, pleasure and peace. Proverbs 3:16 TLB Wisdom gives: A long, good life, Riches, Honor, Pleasure, Peace.

4. Your Wisdom in me makes the hours of my day more profitable and the years of my life more fruitful. Proverbs 9:11 TLB "I, Wisdom, will make the hours of your day more profitable and the years of your life more fruitful."

5. With long life You satisfy me and show me Your salvation. Psalm 91:16 KJV With long life will I satisfy him, and shew him my salvation.

6. You have blessed my eyes to see and my ears to hear. Matthew 13:16 KJV But blessed *are* your eyes, for they see: and your ears, for they hear.

7. Now that I am old and gray, Lord, You have not forsaken me, for I am showing Your strength to this generation and Your power to those who are to come. Psalm 71:18 KJV Now also when I am old and greyheaded, O God, forsake me not; until I have shewed thy strength unto this generation, and thy power to every one that is to come.

8. Thank You, Jesus, that I have Your mega-memory mind working in me, and Your very thoughts thinking through me 1 Corth. 2:16b TLB But, strange as it seems, we Christians actually do have within us a portion of the very thoughts and mind of Christ.

9. I am not timid or fearful, for I have the loving, calm, well-balanced mind You have given me. You have given me the discipline and self-control I need. 2 Timothy 1:7 AMP For God did not give us a spirit of timidity--of cowardice, of craven and cringing fear—but [He has given us a spirit] of power and of love and of calm and well balanced mind and discipline and self control.

HEALTHY AGING

10. I am flourishing like a palm tree. I have been transplanted in Your own garden, Lord, and I am under Your personal care. Even in old age, I am still producing fruit and am vital and green. This honors You and exhibits Your faithful care of me. You are my shelter. There is nothing but goodness in You. <u>Psalm 92:12-15 TLB</u> But the godly shall flourish like palm trees and grow tall as the cedars of Lebanon. For they are transplanted into the Lord's own garden and are under his personal care. Even in old age they will still produce fruit and be vital and green. This honors the Lord and exhibits his faithful care. He is my shelter. There is nothing but goodness in him!

11. You have satisfied my mouth with good things, not only my necessary food, but the kind of food I desire at my personal age, so my youth is now renewed with strength like the eagle's, overcoming and soaring. <u>Psalm 103:5 AMP</u> Who satisfies your mouth [your necessity and desire at your personal age] with good; so that your youth, renewed, is like the eagle's [strong, overcoming, soaring]!

12. Thank You, Lord, I shall come to the grave in full vigor, like sheaves gathered in season. <u>Job 5:26 NIV</u> You will come to the grave in full vigor, like sheaves gathered in season.

13. You have satisfied me early with Your mercy, so I am rejoicing and being glad all my days. <u>Psalm 90:14 KJV</u> O satisfy us early with thy mercy; that we may rejoice and be glad all our days.

14. You have given me added years of life, as rich and full as those of many generations, all packed into one. <u>Psalm 61:6 TLB</u> You will give me added years of life, as rich and full as those of many generations, all packed into one.

15. Lord, You continually bless me with heaven's blessings as well as human joys. I am living to enjoy my grandchildren. <u>Psalm 128:5-6 TLB</u> May the Lord continually bless you with heaven's blessings as well as with human joys. May you live to enjoy your grandchildren! And may God bless Israel!

16. Lord, I do not forget Your teachings, but keep Your commands in my heart, and they prolong my life many years and bring me prosperity. <u>Proverbs 3:1-2 NIV</u> My son, do not forget my teaching, but keep my commands in your heart, for they will prolong your life many years and bring you prosperity.

17. I rejoice, for Your Word has healed me and delivered me from destruction. <u>Psalm 107:20 KJV</u> He sent his word and healed them and delivered them from their destruction.

Ruth Shinness 2539 E. 450 N. Anderson, IN 46012   Web: www.prayerstrategy.com
e-mail <u>PrayerStrategy@juno.com</u> Phone (765) 643-0612 & (765) 642-0623

43

KNOWING JESUS

1. Thank You, Lord, that You have given me the Spirit of wisdom and revelation, so I now know You better. Ephes. 1:17 NIV I keep asking that the God of our Lord Jesus Christ, the glorious Father, may give you the Spirit of wisdom and revelation, so that you may know him better.

2. My heart is flooded with light, so I know something of the future You have called me to share with You. I now understand how great Your power is to help a believer like me. Ephes. 1:18-19 TLB I pray that your hearts will be flooded with light so that you can see something of the future he has called you to share. I want you to realize that God has been made rich because we who are Christ's have been given to him! I pray that you will begin to understand how incredibly great his great power is to help those who believe him.

3. Thank You, Jesus, that I know You and the power of Your resurrection and the fellowship of Your sufferings, and I have been made conformable unto Your death. Philip. 3:10 KJV That I may know him, and the power of his resurrection, and the fellowship of his sufferings, being made conformable unto his death.

4. God, You are pleased to make known to me how great are the riches of the glory of this mystery, which is Christ in me. I am now realizing the glory You have given me. Col. 1:27 NIV To them God has chosen to make known among the Gentiles the glorious riches of this mystery, which is Christ in you, the hope of glory. Isaiah 6:3b KJV The whole earth *is* full of his glory.

5. I have received You, Lord, so now I walk in Your presence, rooted and built up in You and established in the faith, abounding in thanksgiving. Col. 2:6-7 KJV As ye have therefore received Christ Jesus the Lord, *so* walk ye in him: rooted and built up in him, and stablished in the faith, as ye have been taught, abounding therein with thanksgiving.

6. I let heaven fill my thoughts. I do not spend time worrying about things down here. I do not have desires for things down here, for my real life is with You, Christ. Col. 3:2-3 TLB Let heaven fill your thoughts; don't spend your time worrying about things down here. You should have as little desire for this world as a dead person does. Your real life is in heaven with Christ and God.

7. Thank You, Jesus, for letting me live with You now. Romans 6:8 KJV Now if we be dead with Christ, we believe that we shall also live with him.

8. I have been baptized into union with You, Christ, and have clothed myself with Your presence. Galatians 3:27b TLB We who have been baptized into union with Christ are enveloped by him.

KNOWING JESUS

9. Jesus, when You died, my sin-loving nature was buried with You, and when You were brought to life, You gave me Your wonderful life to enjoy. Romans 6:4 TLB Your old sin-loving nature was buried with him by baptism when he died; and when God the Father, with glorious power, brought him back to life again, you were given his wonderful new life to enjoy.

10. I love others and because I love, I am born of You, God, and know You. 1 John 4:7-8 KJV Beloved, let us love one another: for love is of God; and every one that loveth is born of God, and knoweth God. He that loveth not knoweth not God; for God is love.

11. Lord, You are my inheritance, my prize, my food and drink, my highest joy! I always think of You, Lord. Because You are so near, I need never stumble or fall. Psalm 16:5,8 TLB The Lord himself is my inheritance, my prize. He is my food and drink, my highest joy! I am always thinking of the Lord; because he is so near, I never need to stumble or to fall.

12. Thank You, Lord, You have given me leaders to build me up and to help me know how to minister. I have come into the unity of the faith with others and the knowledge of You. Jesus, I am now filled full of You. Ephes. 4:11-13 KJV And he gave some, apostles; and some, prophets; and some, evangelists; and some, pastors and teachers; For the perfecting of the saints, for the work of the ministry, for the edifying of the body of Christ: Till we all come in the unity of the faith, and of the knowledge of the Son of God, unto a perfect man, unto the measure of the stature of the fullness of Christ.

13. I now have more of Your kindness and peace, because I have learned to know You better. You have given me, through Your power, everything I need to live a truly good life, for You now share Your goodness and glory with me. 2 Peter 1:2-3 TLB Do you want more and more of God's kindness and peace? Then learn to know him better and better. For as you know him better, he will give you, through his great power, everything you need for living a truly good life: he even shares his own glory and his own goodness with us!

14. I praise You that I have eternal life, which means I now know You, God, and Your Son whom You have sent. John 17:3 KJV And this is life eternal, that they may know thee the only true God, and Jesus Christ, whom thou hast sent.

15. You have chosen me to come and live with You within the Holy Tabernacle courts. What joys I have among all the good things there! Psalm 65:4 TLB How greatly to be envied are those you have chosen to come and live with you within the holy tabernacle courts! What joys await us among all the good things there.

Ruth Shinness 2539 E. 450 N. Anderson, IN 46012   Web: www.prayerstrategy.com
e-mail PrayerStrategy@juno.com Phone (765) 643-0612 & (765) 642-0623

45

LOST

1. They have repented and their sins are blotted out, and they are refreshing themselves in Your presence, Lord. Acts 3:19 KJV Repent ye therefore, and be converted, that your sins may be blotted out, when the times of refreshing shall come from the presence of the Lord.

2. Because of what You have done, Jesus, God has ended their bondage. He has broken the slave yoke off their neck. Isaiah 10:27 TLB On that day God will end the bondage of his people. He will break the slave-yoke off their necks and destroy it as decreed.

3. They have returned to You, Lord, and You have healed them. Hosea 6:1 KJV Come, and let us return unto the LORD: for he hath torn, and he will heal us; he hath smitten, and he will bind us up.

4. They cried to You, Lord, in their troubles, and now You have heard and delivered them. Psalm 107:1 TLB Then they cried to the Lord in their troubles, and he helped them and delivered them.

5. Thank You, that You have drawn them to Yourself, Lord, and raised them up in this day. John 6:44 KJV No man can come to me, except the Father which hath sent me draw him: and I will raise him up at the last day.

6. Thank You, Lord, that the Comforter has come, and he has reproved them of sin, and of righteousness and of judgment and they now believe on You. John 16:7-9 KJV Nevertheless I tell you the truth; It is expedient for you that I go away: for if I go not away, the Comforter will not come unto you; but if I depart, I will send him unto you. And when he is come, he will reprove the world of sin, and of righteousness, and of judgment: Of sin, because they believe not on me.

7. They pray, seek Your face, and turn from their sins, so You have heard from heaven, forgiving their sins and healing their land. 2 Chron. 7:14 NIV If my people, who are called by my name, will humble themselves and pray and seek my face and turn from their wicked ways, then will I hear from heaven and will forgive their sin and will heal their land.

8. You, God have commanded Your light to shine in their heart, to give them the knowledge of Your glory in the face of Jesus Christ. 2 Corth 4:6 KJV For God, who commanded the light to shine out of darkness, hath shined in our hearts, to give the light of the knowledge of the glory of God in the face of Jesus Christ.

9. They were lost and now they are found. Luke 15:32 TLB He was lost and is found.

Ruth Shinness 2539 E. 450 N Anderson, IN 46012-9518   Web: www.prayerstrategy.com
e-mail PrayerStrategy@juno.com   Phone (765) 643-0612 & (765) 642-0623

LOST

10. Our most gracious Lord, I am so grateful to You for bringing repentance to their heart. My joy overflows, for You have put the robe of righteousness on them, put a ring on their finger to marry them to You and sandals on their feet so that now they walk the paths of life and light. I rejoice that they now eat the richest of food at Your banquet table. I celebrate that they have come home; were lost and now they are found. Luke 15:21-24 NIV The son said to him, "Father, I have sinned against heaven and against you. I am no longer worthy to be called your son." But the father said to his servant, "Quick! Bring the best robe and put on him. Put a ring on his finger and sandals on his feet. Bring the fatted calf and kill it. For this son of mine was dead and is alive again, he was lost and is found." So they began to celebrate.

11. They have sought You, Lord, and You have come and have rained righteousness upon them. Hosea 10:12 KJV Sow to yourselves in righteousness, reap in mercy; break up your fallow ground: for it is time to seek the LORD, till he come and rain righteousness upon you.

12. The time has been fulfilled for them; they have repented and are believing the gospel, and now the kingdom of God has come to them. Mark 1:15 KJV And saying, The time is fulfilled, and the kingdom of God is at hand: repent ye, and believe the gospel.

13. The gospel is no longer hidden to them, their minds are no longer blinded, for the light of Your glorious gospel, Christ, shines on them. 2 Corth. 4:3-4 KJV But if our gospel be hid, it is hid to them that are lost: In whom the god of this world hath blinded the minds of them which believe not, lest the light of the glorious gospel of Christ, who is the image of God, should shine unto them.

14. They are new creatures in You, Christ; their old ways have passed from them and all things in their life have become new in Your ways. 2 Corth. 5:17 KJV Therefore if any man be in Christ, he is a new creature: old things are passed away; behold, all things are become new.

15. They have now been rewarded for seeking You, Lord. Hebrews 11:6 NKJV But without faith it is impossible to please Him, for he who comes to God must believe that He is, and that He is a rewarder of those who diligently seek Him.

16. Lord, You are in the midst of them and You are mighty. You have saved them and are rejoicing over them with joy. You rest in Your love for them, rejoicing over them with singing. Zeph. 3:17 KJV The Lord thy God in the midst of thee is mighty; he will save, he will rejoice over thee with joy; he will rest in his love, he will joy over thee with singing.

LOVE

1. As I now obey Your commandment to love others, the darkness in my life has disappeared and the new light of life in You Christ, now shines in me. 1 John 3:8b TLB As we obey this commandment, to love one another, the darkness in our lives disappears and the new light of life in Christ shines in.

2. Thank You, Lord, that You have made my love to grow and overflow to others everywhere, just as their love flows toward me. 1 Thes. 3:12 TLB And may the Lord make your love to grow and overflow to each other and to everyone else, just as our love does toward you.

3. Lord, You have taught me that Your love in me never gives up. I care for others more than myself. I now have peace and contentment with what I do have. 1 Corth. 13:4a MES Love never gives up. Love cares for others than for self. Love doesn't want what it doesn't have.

4. I don't have the "big head", force my ideas on others, and always have a "me first" attitude. I don't fly off the handle, keep score of the sins of others, or revel in others "down moments" but I love to bring forth the beauty of Your truth. 1 Corth. 13: 5-6 MES Doesn't have a swelled head, Doesn't force itself on others, Isn't always "me first," Doesn't fly off the handle, Doesn't keep score of the sins of others, Doesn't revel when others grovel, Takes pleasure in the flowering of truth.

5. I have learned to put up with anything, trusting You always, looking for the best. I set myself never to look back and I keep going to the end. 1 Corth. 13:7 MES Puts up with anything, Trusts God always, Always looks for the best, Never looks back, But keeps going to the end.

6. Because Your love is in me and for me, Lord, I have true affection for You and for others. 1 Corth. 13:13b TLB Love, true affection for God and man, growing out of God's love for and in us.

7. No matter what happens, Lord, I hold my head up high, and I know that all is well; for I know how dearly You love me. You have given me the Holy Spirit to fill my heart with the warmth of Your love. Romans 5:5 TLB Then, when that happens, we are able to hold our heads high no matter what happens and know that all is well, for we know how dearly God loves us, and we feel this warm love everywhere within us because God has given us the Holy Spirit to fill our hearts with his love.

8. Lord, because You are love, I am like You, loving others. 1 John 4:7 KJV Beloved, let us love one another: for love is of God.

Ruth Shinness 2539 E. 450 N Anderson, IN 46012-9518 Web: www.prayerstrategy.com
e-mail PrayerStrategy@juno.com Phone (765) 643-0612 & (765) 642-0623

LOVE

9. Lord, I thank You that my love now flows more and more to others and at the same time I keep growing in spiritual knowledge and insights. I now see clearly between right and wrong, recognizing the highest and the best in everyone. Philip. 1:9-11 TLB My prayer for you is that you will overflow more and more with love for others, and at the same time keep on growing in spiritual knowledge and insight, for I want you always to see clearly the difference between right and wrong, and to be inwardly clean, no one being able to criticize you from now until our Lord returns.

10. I am so glad, Lord, that You have directed my heart to realize and to show Your love to others. 2 Thes. 3:5b AMP Now may the Lord direct your hearts into [realizing and showing] the love of God.

11. I am keeping myself in Your love, Lord. Jude 1:21 KJV Keep yourselves in the love of God, looking for the mercy of our Lord Jesus Christ unto eternal life.

12. Thank You, Lord, that I have learned to love by covering and forgiving offenses. I am not cutting off friendships by repeating stories about them. Proverbs 17:9 KJV He that covereth a transgression seeketh love; but he that repeateth a matter separateth very friends.

13. I am so glad that nothing can separate me from Your love, Lord. Death can't and life can't. The angels won't, and the powers of hell itself cannot keep Your love away. My fears for today, worries about tomorrow, or where we are--high above the sky or in the deepest ocean--nothing will ever be able to separate me from Your love demonstrated by You, Lord, when You died for me. Romans 8:38-39 TLB For I am convinced that nothing can ever separate us from his love. Death can't, and life can't. The angels won't, and all the powers of hell itself cannot keep God's love away. Our fears for today, our worries about tomorrow, or where we are--high above the sky, or in the deepest ocean--nothing will ever be able to separate us from the love of God demonstrated by our Lord Jesus Christ when he died for us.

14. Lord, I have set myself not to hate others, for I don't want to walk in darkness. I love others, so that I may abide in Your light and love. In this way I have eyes to see the right path for me. 1 John 2:9-11 KJV He that saith he is in the light, and hateth his brother, is in darkness even until now. He that loveth his brother abideth in the light, and there is none occasion of stumbling in him. But he that hateth his brother is in darkness, and walketh in darkness, and knoweth not whither he goeth, because that darkness hath blinded his eyes.

15. You, Lord, have made me increase and abound in love toward others. 1 Thes. 3:12 KJV And the Lord make you increase and abound in love one toward another.

Ruth Shinness 2539 E. 450 N. Anderson, IN 46012 Web: www.prayerstrategy.com
e-mail PrayerStrategy@juno.com Phone (765) 643-0612 & (765) 642-0623

49

MEN

1. I succeed because You, Lord, have made me to succeed. Romans 4:4 TEV
He shall succeed because God is able to make him to succeed.

2. I am kind to my family and think of ways to please them and speak good words to them, and my family wants to be my servant forever. 2 Chron. 10:7 NKJV And they spoke to him, saying, "If you are kind to these people, and please them, and speak good words to them, they will be your servants forever."

3. The hand of the Lord is with me to give me one heart to do the commandments. 2 Chron. 30:12 NIV Also in Judah the hand of God was on the people to give them unity of mind to carry out what the king and his officials had ordered, following the word of the LORD.

4. Lord, You have given me responsibility over my people; whatever I say will be done; none will be able to stop me. You have made me a strong and steady peg to support my own family; You load me with responsibility and I am an honor to my family name. Isaiah 22:22-23 TLB "I will give him responsibility over all my people; whatever he says will be done; none will be able to stop him. I will make of him a strong and steady peg to support my people; they will load him with responsibility, and he will be an honor to his family name."

5. Thank You that You are with my mouth, teaching me what I should say. Exodus 4:12 NKJV Now therefore, go, and I will be with your mouth and teach you what you shall say.

6. I love my wife as You, Christ, love the Church and gave Yourself up for her. I nourish her and carefully protect her and I cherish her just like You do the Church. Ephes. 5:25 NKJV Husbands, love your wives, just as Christ also loved the church and gave Himself for her.

7. I command my household to keep Your ways, Lord; to do justice and judgment, so that I have Abraham's blessings on me and my family. Genesis 18:19 KJV For I know him, that he will command his children and his household after him, and they shall keep the way of the LORD, to do justice and judgment; that the LORD may bring upon Abraham that which he hath spoken of him. (We are Abraham's seed, heirs according to the promise).

8. Lord, so my prayers won't be hindered, I am thoughtful of my wife and treat her with respect, for we are partners and heirs with You. 1 Peter 3:7 NIV Husbands, in the same way be considerate as you live with your wives, and treat them with respect as the weaker partner and as heirs with you of the gracious gift of life, so that nothing will hinder your prayers.

Ruth Shinness 2539 E. 450 N Anderson, IN 46012-9518 Web: www.prayerstrategy.com
e-mail PrayerStrategy@juno.com Phone (765) 643-0612 & (765) 642-0623

MEN

9. My heart is in Your hands, Lord, and You are turning my heart where You want to. <u>Proverbs 21:1 KJV</u> The king's heart is in the hand of the LORD, as the rivers of water: he turneth it whithersoever he will.

10. I am thankful that through Jesus Your grace, God, is upon me and I am enriched in every way--in all speaking and all knowledge. <u>1 Corth 1:4,5</u> <u>NIV</u> I always thank God for you because of his grace given you in Christ Jesus. For in him you have been enriched in every way--in all your speaking and in all your knowledge.

11. Praise You, God, for I fear and trust You so that I am blessed beyond expression. Yes, I am happy because I love doing Your commands. <u>Psalm</u> <u>112:1 TLB</u> Praise the Lord! For all who fear God and trust in him are blessed beyond expression. Yes, happy is the man who delights in doing his commands.

12. Thank You that my children are honored everywhere, for good men's children have a special heritage. <u>Psalm 112:2 TLB</u> His children shall be honored everywhere, for good men's sons have a special heritage.

13. I am wealthy and my good deeds are never to be forgotten. <u>Psalm 112:3</u> <u>TLB</u> He himself shall be wealthy, and his good deeds will never be forgotten.

14. When darkness overtakes me, Your light comes bursting in. I am kind and merciful and all goes well for me for I conduct my business fairly. <u>Psalm 112:4-5 TLB</u> When darkness overtakes him light will come bursting in. He is kind and merciful--and all goes well for the generous man who conducts his business fairly.

15. I am not overthrown by evil circumstances. Everyone is impressed by Your constant care of me, God. I do not fear bad news, nor live in dread of what might happen; for I know that You are taking care of me, and that is why I am not afraid, but can calmly face my foes. <u>Psalm 112:6-8 TLB</u> Such a man will not be overthrown by evil circumstances. God's constant care of him will make a deep impression on all who see it. He does not fear bad news, nor live in dread of what may happen. For he is settled in his mind that Jehovah will take care of him. That is why he is not afraid but can calmly face his foes.

16. I give generously to those in need, and my deeds will never be forgotten. I have influence and honor. <u>Psalm 112:9 TLB</u> He gives generously to those in need. His deeds will never be forgotten. He shall have influence and honor.

17. I am now living joyfully with the wife You have given me, who I love all the days of my life. <u>Eccles 9:9 KJV</u> Live joyfully with the wife thou lovest all the days of the life of the vanity, which he hath given thee under the sun.

PERFECT IN GOD'S EYES
Freedom From Sin and Gluttony

1. Thank You, God, that my body is Your temple and wonderfully made by You. You dwell in me. I set myself to glorify You in my body and in my Spirit. 1 Corth. 6:19-20 NKJV Do you not know that your body is the temple of the Holy Spirit who is in you, whom you have from God, and you are not your own? For you were bought at a price; therefore glorify God in your body and in your spirit, which are God's.

2. Lord, You are my prize; I have inherited You. You are my food, my drink, and my highest joy. Psalm 16:5 TLB The Lord himself is my inheritance, my prize. He is my food and drink, my highest joy! He guards all that is mine.

3. Thank You, Lord, that I am not timid or fearful, for I have the loving, calm, well-balanced mind You have given me. I now have the discipline and the self-control I need. 2 Timothy 1:7 AMP For God did not give us a spirit of timidity--of cowardice, of craven and cringing fear--but [He has given us a spirit] of power and of love and of calm and well balanced mind and discipline and self control.

4. I am chosen by You, God, to stand before You without a single fault, perfect in body, mind and spirit, covered by Your love. Ephes. 1:4 TLB Long ago, even before he made the world, God chose us to be his very own through what Christ would do for us; he decided then to make us holy in his eyes, without a single fault--we who stand before him covered with his love.

5. I now know, Lord, that sin and gluttony no longer have the rule in my life, for I am not under the law but under grace. Romans 6:14 KJV For sin shall not have dominion over you: for ye are not under the law, but under grace.

6. Since You dwell in me, Lord, I no longer need to set my mind on what my nature desires, but I now live according to the Spirit, having my mind set on what the Spirit desires. Romans 8:5 NIV Those who live according to the sinful nature have their minds set on what that nature desires; but those who live in accordance with the Spirit have their minds set on what the Spirit desires.

7. I am controlled by my new nature, for Your Spirit lives in me. Romans 8:9 The Book You are controlled by your new nature if you have the Spirit of God living in you.

8. I am more than a conqueror through You, Jesus, for You love me. Romans 8:37 KJV Nay, in all these things we are more than conquerors through him that loved us.

9. When I eat or drink, or whatever I do, I do it all to the Glory of You, God. 1 Corth. 10:31 KJV Whether therefore ye eat or drink or whatever ye do, do all to the glory of God.

Ruth Shinness 2539 E. 450 N Anderson, IN 46012-9518 Web: www.prayerstrategy.com
e-mail PrayerStrategy@juno.com Phone (765) 643-0612 & (765) 642-0623

PERFECT IN GOD'S EYES
Freedom From Sin and Gluttony

10. Thank You, Lord, that when I eat the good food You have given me, my mouth is satisfied. My youth is now renewed like the eagle's--strong, overcoming and soaring. Psalm 103:5 AMP Who satisfies your mouth [your necessity and your desire at your personal age] with good; so that your youth, renewed, is like the eagle's [strong, overcoming, soaring]!

11. I am glad, Lord; I do not want more food than I need. Psalm 23:1 KJV The LORD *is* my shepherd; I shall not want.

12. I have wrapped myself up in Your presence, Jesus, and that way I am not thinking about how to gratify the desires of my sinful nature. Romans 13:14 NIV Rather, clothe yourselves with the Lord Jesus Christ, and do not think about how to gratify the desires of the sinful nature.

13. Jesus, You are the true bread, and I now feed on You. Your presence has given life to me. John 6:33 NIV For the bread of God is he who comes down from heaven and gives life to the world.

14. Now that I have come to You, Jesus, I am not hungry as before. John 6:35 NIV Then Jesus declared, "I am the bread of life. He who comes to me will never go hungry, and he who believes in me will never be thirsty."

15. I now live by Your Spirit, Jesus, and I do not gratify the desires of the flesh. Galatians 5:16 NIV So I say, live by the Spirit, and you will not gratify the desires of the sinful nature.

16. Christ, You have triumphed over every defeat in my life, so now no matter where I go, I tell others what You have done, Lord, and spread the Gospel like a sweet perfume. 2 Cor. 2:14 TLB But thanks be to God! For through what Christ has done, he has triumphed over us so that now wherever we go he uses us to tell others about the Lord and to spread the Gospel like a sweet perfume.

17. My old evil desires were nailed to the cross with You, Jesus. The part of me that loved to sin was fatally wounded and crushed, so my sin-loving body is no longer under the control of sin. Romans 6:6 TLB Your old evil desires were nailed to the cross with him; that part of you that loves to sin was crushed and fatally wounded, so that your sin-loving body is no longer under sin's control, no longer needs to be a slave to sin.

18. Thank You for You do not lead me into temptation, but have delivered me from evil. Luke 11:4b KJV And lead us not into temptation; but deliver us from evil.

Ruth Shinness 2539 E. 450 N. Anderson, IN 46012 Web: www.prayerstrategy.com
e-mail PrayerStrategy@juno.com Phone (765) 643-0612 & (765) 642-0623

53

PROSPER

1. Above all things, I am prospering and in health, and at the same time my soul is prospering. <u>3 John 1:2 KJV</u> Beloved, I wish above all things that thou mayest prosper and be in health, even as thy soul prospereth.

2. You, God, have supplied all my needs according to Your riches in glory by Christ Jesus. <u>Philip. 4:19 KJV</u> But my God shall supply all your need according to his riches in glory by Christ Jesus.

3. Because You are my shepherd I do not want for any good thing. <u>Psalm 23:1 KJV</u> The Lord is my Shepherd: I shall not want.

4. I fear You, Lord, and delight in Your commands, so wealth and riches are in my house. <u>Psalm 112:1,3 NIV</u> Blessed is the man who fears the LORD, who finds great delight in his commands. Wealth and riches are in his house.

5. Because I bring my tithes into the church, You have opened the windows of heaven and have poured more blessings on me than I can even contain. You have rebuked the devourer of my money and blessings. People see me and call me blessed; both me and my land are a delight. <u>Malachi 3:10, 11a, 12 KJV</u> Bring ye all the tithes into the storehouse, that there may be meat in mine house, and prove me now herewith, saith the LORD of hosts, if I will not open you the windows of heaven, and pour you out a blessing, that there shall not be room enough to receive it. I will rebuke the devourer for your sake.All the nations shall call you blessed and ye shall be a delightsome land, saith the Lord of host.

6. You have given me power to get wealth, and that fulfills Your promise to my ancestors. <u>Deut. 8:18 TLB</u> Always remember that it is the Lord your God who gives you power to become rich, and he does it to fulfill his promise to your ancestors.

7. I am truly rich with Your blessings, Lord, and You add no sorrow to it, neither does toiling increase it. <u>Proverbs 10:22 AMP</u> The blessings of the Lord, it makes [truly] rich, and He adds no sorrow with it, neither does toiling increase it.

8. I enjoy all the things You have richly given me. <u>1 Tim. 6:17b KJV</u> God, giveth us richly all things to enjoy.

9. Because I love You, You have caused me to inherit wealth; You have filled my treasures. My heart is full of thanksgiving. <u>Proverbs 8:21 NKJV</u> That I may cause those who love me to inherit wealth, that I may fill their treasures.

10. I owe no man anything, except my gift of love to them. <u>Romans.13:8 KJV</u> Owe no man anything, but to love one another.

Ruth Shinness 2539 E. 450 N Anderson, IN 46012-9518 Web: www.prayerstrategy.com
e-mail PrayerStrategy@juno.com Phone (765) 643-0612 & (765) 642-0623

PROSPER

11. I give away money and things and become richer. <u>Proverbs 11:24 TLB</u> It is possible to give away and become richer! It is also possible to hold on too tightly and lose everything.

12. Everything I set my hand to is blessed. I am blessed in the land You have given me. <u>Deut.</u> 28:8 KJV The LORD shall command the blessing upon thee in thy storehouses, and in all that thou settest thine hand unto; and he shall bless thee in the land which the LORD thy God giveth thee.

13. I bless You, Lord, for teaching me to profit and leading me in the way I should go. <u>Isaiah 48:17 KJV</u> Thus saith the LORD, thy Redeemer, the Holy One of Israel; I am the LORD thy God which teacheth thee to profit, which leadeth thee by the way that thou shouldest go.

14. I shout for joy and am glad, for I favor Your righteous cause; I say continually, "Let the Lord be magnified who has pleasure in my prosperity." <u>Psalm 35:27 KJV</u> Let them shout for joy, and be glad, that favour my righteous cause: yea, let them say continually, Let the LORD be magnified, which hath pleasure in the prosperity of his servant.

15. You have given me the treasures of darkness and hidden riches in secret places so that I know that You are the LORD who calls me by name. <u>Isaiah 45:3 KJV</u> And I will give thee the treasures of darkness, and hidden riches of secret place, that thou mayest know that I, the LORD, which call thee by thy name, am the God of Israel.

16. I have given, so now I am receiving back, good measure, pressed down and running over from others. <u>Luke 6:38 KJV</u> Give, and it shall be given unto you; good measure, pressed down, and shaken together, and running over, shall men give into your bosom. For with the same measure that ye mete withal it shall be measured to you again.

17. Christ, You have made wisdom come me, and now I have a good life with riches, honor and peace. <u>Proverbs 3:16 TLB</u> Wisdom gives: A long good life, riches, honor, pleasure, peace. <u>1Corth. 1:30 KJV</u> But of him are ye in Christ Jesus, who of God is made unto us wisdom, and righteousness, and sanctification, and redemption.

18. You have remembered me, Lord, while You blessed and saved Your people. I now share in Your chosen ones' prosperity and rejoice in all their joys, and receive the same glory You gave them. <u>Psalm 106:4-5 TLB</u> Remember me too, O Lord, while You are blessing and saving Your people. Let me share in Your chosen ones' prosperity and rejoice in all their joys, and receive the glory You give to them.

SAVE CHILDREN

1. I do not labor in vain nor bring forth my children for trouble, for I am a descendant of the blessed of you Lord, and all my offspring with me. Isaiah 65:23 NKJV They shall not labor in vain, Nor bring forth children for trouble; For they shall be the descendants of the blessed of the LORD, And their offspring with them.

2. You have not forsaken me, Lord, for I am the work of Your hands. You have made perfect everything that concerns me. Psalm 138:8 KJV The LORD will perfect that which concerneth me: thy mercy, O LORD, endureth forever: forsake not the works of thine own hands.

3. These children are keeping their father's God-given commandments, forsaking not the law of God taught by their mother. Wherever they go the Word of their parents' God is leading them; when they sleep, this Word keeps them: when they wake up, this Word is talking to them. The commandment is a lamp, the whole teaching of the law is light, and the reproofs of discipline are a way of life to keep them from a wrong sexual life. Proverbs 6:20,22-24 AMP My son, keep your father's [God-given] commandments and forsake not the law of [God] your mother [taught you]. When you go, they [the word of your parents' God] shall lead you: when you sleep, they shall keep you: and when you waken they shall talk to you. For the commandment is a lamp, and the whole teaching [of the law] is light, and reproofs of discipline are a way of life, to keep you from the evil woman, from the flattery of the tongue of the loose woman.

4. You, God, have poured Your spirit upon my children and Your blessing upon my offspring. They have sprung up as among the grass, as a willow by the watercourse. Isaiah 44:3-4 KJV For I will pour water upon him that is thirsty, and floods upon the dry ground: I will pour my spirit upon thy seed, and my blessing upon thine offspring: And they shall spring up as among the grass, as willows by the watercourses.

5. Thank You, Lord, that Your spirit is on me, and the words You have put in my mouth shall not depart from my mouth or the mouth of my children or the mouth of my children's children. Isaiah 59:21 KJV As for me, this is my covenant with them, saith the LORD; My spirit that is upon thee, and my words which I have put in thy mouth, shall not depart out of thy mouth, nor out of the mouth of thy seed, nor out of the mouth of thy seed's seed, saith the LORD, from henceforth and for ever.

6. You have cleansed my heart and the hearts of my children and grandchildren, so we love You with all our hearts and souls. Deut. 30:6 The Book He will cleanse your hearts and the hearts of your children, and your children's children so that you will love the Lord your God with all your hearts and souls.

7. The fruit of my body is blessed. Deut. 28:4 NKJV Blessed shall be the fruit of your body.

Ruth Shinness 2539 E. 450 N Anderson, IN 46012-9518 Web: www.prayerstrategy.com
e-mail PrayerStrategy@juno.com Phone (765) 643-0612 & (765) 642-0623

SAVE CHILDREN

8. My children are taught of You, Lord, and obedient to Your will, and great is the peace and undisturbed composure of my children. They are established in conformity with Your will and order. They are far from destruction, for we do not fear, for we know that no weapon formed against them shall prosper, and every tongue that shall rise against them in judgment We shall show to be wrong. This peace and triumph over opposition is our heritage as Your servants, Lord. Isaiah 54:13,14,17 AMP And all your children shall be [taught of the Lord and obedient to His will], and great shall be the peace and undisturbed composure of your children. You shall establish yourself in righteousness (rightness, in conformity with God's will and order): you shall be far from even the thought of oppression or destruction, for you shall not fear, and from terror, for it shall not come near you. No weapon formed against you shall prosper, and every tongue that shall rise against you in judgment you shall show to be wrong. This [peace, righteousness, security, triumph over opposition] is the heritage of the servant of the servants of the Lord.

9. Discretion is preserving my children; understanding keeps them, to deliver them from the way of the evil man who leaves the path of uprightness to walk in ways of darkness. Proverbs 2:11-14 KJV Discretion shall preserve thee, understanding shall keep thee: To deliver thee from the way of the evil man, from the man that speaketh froward things; Who leave the paths of uprightness, to walk in the ways of darkness; Who rejoice to do evil, and delight in the frowardness of the wicked.

10. My children are having no fellowship with the unfruitful works of darkness, but rather are reproving them. All are ashamed to even speak of those dark things that are done by them in secret. Ephes. 5:11-12 KJV And have no fellowship with the unfruitful works of darkness, but rather reprove them. For it is a shame even to speak of those things which are done of them in secret.

11. They are abstaining from fleshly lusts which war against the flesh, and are conducting themselves honorably among people; and by their good works, which people observe, glorify God. 1 Peter 2:11-12 NKJV Beloved, I beg you as sojourners and pilgrims, abstain from fleshly lusts which war against the soul, having your conduct honorable among the Gentiles, that when they speak against you as evildoers, they may, by your good works which they observe, glorify God in the day of visitation.

12. They are doing no iniquity, but are walking in Your way, Lord. Psalm 119:3 NKJV They also do no iniquity: they walk in his ways.

13. Look how You have cleansed their ways, for they have taken heed to Your Word. Psalm 119:9 KJV Wherewithal shall a young man cleanse his way? by taking heed thereto according to thy word.

Ruth Shinness 2539 E. 450 N. Anderson, IN 46012   Web: www.prayerstrategy.com
e-mail PrayerStrategy@juno.com Phone (765) 643-0612 & (765) 642-0623

57

SOUND MIND

1. I now forgive anyone who has brought any negative influence into my life and I now set them free for You to work Your best in and through their lives. Col. 3:13 NIV Bear with each other and forgive whatever grievances you may have against one another. Forgive as the Lord forgave you.

2. I am not adjusting my life to the culture around me; but instead, I am fixing my attention on You, God. In this way You bring out the best in me and have developed me into a well-formed mature person. You have changed me from the inside out. Romans 13:2 MES Don't become so well adjusted to your culture that you fit into it without even thinking. Instead, fix your attention on God. You'll be changed from the inside out.

3. You are so kind to take away all of my sins by the blood of Your Son, by whom I am saved. I now stand before You covered with Your love. Ephes. 1:7,4b TLB So overflowing is his kindness toward us that he took away all our sins through the blood of his Son, by whom we are saved. We stand before Him covered with his love.

4. I know, Lord, that good is now coming forth in every and all parts of my life, because I am one of those who loves You. You have called me and are working Your good purpose in my life. Romans 8:28 NIV And we know that in all things God works for the good of those who love him, who have been called according to his purpose.

5. I am always full of joy in You, Lord. I say it again, I rejoice over and over again, thinking about You during each day. Philip. 4:4 TLB Always be full of joy in the Lord; I say it again, rejoice!

6. Now I don't worry about anything anymore; instead, God, I tell You all my needs and I keep thanking You for all the answers. Now my mind is filled with Your peace. This peace is keeping my thoughts and my heart quiet and at rest as I trust in You. Philip. 4:6-7 TLB Don't worry about anything; instead, pray about everything; tell God your needs, and don't forget to thank him for his answers. If you do this, you will experience God's peace, which is far more wonderful than the human mind can understand. His peace will keep your thoughts and your hearts quiet and at rest as you trust in Christ Jesus.

7. Lord, I now have the power to fix my thoughts on what is true and good and right. I am always thinking about things that are pure and lovely. I am dwelling on the fine, good things in others. I am thinking about all I can praise You for and be glad about. Philip 4:8 TLB Fix your thoughts on what is true and good and right. Think about things that are pure and lovely, and dwell on the fine, good things in others. Think about all you can praise God for and be glad about.

Ruth Shinness 2539 E. 450 N Anderson, IN 46012-9518 Web: www.prayerstrategy.com
e-mail PrayerStrategy@juno.com Phone (765) 643-0612 & (765) 642-0623

SOUND MIND

8. Thank You that I have the mind of Christ, Your thoughts thinking through me. 1 Corth. 2:16 b KJV But we have the mind of Christ.

9. Lord, in the midst of the many thoughts within me, Your comforts delight my soul. Psalm 94:19 KJV In the multitude of my thoughts within me thy comforts delight my soul.

10. I am now keeping my mind in perfect peace, O Lord, for my mind is stayed on You, trusting in You. Isaiah 26:3 NKJV You will keep him in perfect peace, Whose mind is stayed on You, Because he trusts in You.

11. I no longer have my mind on the enemy, Lord, but I stay my mind on You and Your word. Isaiah 10:20 KJV And it shall come to pass in that day, that the remnant of Israel, and such as are escaped of the house of Jacob, shall no more again stay upon him that smote them; but shall stay upon the LORD, the Holy One of Israel, in truth.

12. Thank You forever, Lord, that I am no longer timid nor afraid of people, for You have given me the spirit of power. You have given me the spirit of love. You have given me a calm and well-balanced mind. I now have discipline and self-control. 2 Timothy 1:7 AMP For God did not give us a spirit of timidity -- of cowardice, of craven and cringing and fawning fear -- but [He has given us a spirit] of power and of love and of calm and well-balanced mind and discipline and self control.

13. Lord, You have given me mighty weapons to pull down strongholds in my mind. Now I have the power to bring every thought to line up with what the Word says is already mine or is God's will for me. 2 Corth. 10:4-5 KJV (For the weapons of our warfare are not carnal, but mighty through God to the pulling down of strong holds;) Casting down imaginations, and every high thing that exalteth itself against the knowledge of God, and bringing into captivity every thought to the obedience of Christ.

14. I am in You, Christ, so I am a new creation. The old ways of my life have passed away; everything about my life has become new and all these new ways are of You. 2 Cor. 5:17 NKJV Therefore, if anyone is in Christ, he is a new creation; old things have passed away; behold, all things have become new.

15. The day is now here, Jesus, that You have taken the burden from my shoulder and the yoke from my neck, and the yoke has been destroyed because of Your anointing that is upon me. Isaiah 10:27 KJV And it shall come to pass in that day, that his burden shall be taken away from off thy shoulder, and his yoke from off thy neck, and the yoke shall be destroyed because of the anointing.

Ruth Shinness 2539 E. 450 N. Anderson, IN 46012 Web: www.prayerstrategy.com
e-mail PrayerStrategy@juno.com Phone (765) 643-0612 & (765) 642-0623

59

STRENGTH

1.Thank You, God, You are my strong fortress; You make me safe.
2 Samuel 22:33 TLB   God is my strong fortress; He has made me safe.

2. You command my strength to me, O God, and You have strengthen all that You have done for me.   Psalm 68:28 NKJV   Your God has commanded your strength; Strengthen, O God, what You have done for us.

3. You have given unto me out of Your glorious unlimited resources to be strengthened with might through Your Spirit in the inner man.   Ephes. 3:16 NKJV   That He would grant you, according to the riches of His glory, to be strengthened with might through His Spirit in the inner man.

4. Lord, because I know that You are my light, You are my salvation, I do not fear anymore. Because You are the strength of my life, I am not afraid of anyone.   Psalm 27:1 KJV   The LORD is my light and my salvation; whom shall I fear? the LORD is the strength of my life; of whom shall I be afraid?

5. You have given strength to me; You have blessed me with peace.   Psalm 29:11 KJV   The LORD will give strength unto his people; the LORD will bless his people with peace.

6. In the very day that I cried out, You answered me and You have made me bold with strength in my soul.   Psalm 138:3 NKJV   In the day when I cried out, You answered me, And made me bold with strength in my soul.

7. I bless You, Lord, for You are my strength. You have taught my hands to war and my fingers to fight.   Psalm 144:1 KJV   Blessed be the LORD my strength, which teacheth my hands to war, and my fingers to fight.

8. Yes, I have returned to You, Lord, and I am resting in You, for that is the way You said I would be saved; my quietness, my trusting confidence is my strength. Yes, so I do this now.   Isaiah 30:15 AMP   For thus said the Lord God, the Holy One of Israel, In returning to Me and resting in Me you shall be saved; in quietness and in (trusting) confidence shall be your strength.

9. When I am faint, You give me power. When I have no might You increase my strength.   Isaiah 40:29 KJV   He giveth power to the faint; and to them that have no might he increaseth strength.

10. I am strong!   Joel 3:10 KJV   Let the weak say I am strong.

Ruth Shinness 2539 E. 450 N Anderson, IN 46012-9518   Web: www.prayerstrategy.com
e-mail PrayerStrategy@juno.com Phone (765) 643-0612 & (765) 642-0623

STRENGTH

11. Lord, You fill me with strength and You protect me wherever I go. You give me sure-footedness like a mountain goat upon the crags. You lead me safely along tops of the cliffs. You prepare me for battle and give me strength to draw the iron bow! <u>Psalm 18:32 The Book</u> He fills me with strength and protects me wherever I go. He gives me sure-footedness of a mountain goat upon the crags. He leads me safely along the tops of the cliffs. He prepares me for battle and gives me strength to draw the iron bow!

12. You have given me Your salvation as a shield. Your right hand, Lord, supports me; Your gentleness has made me great. You make wide steps beneath my feet so I need never slip. <u>Psalm 18:35 The Book</u> You have given me your salvation as a shield. Your right hand, O Lord supports me; your gentleness has made me great. You have made wide steps beneath my feet so I need never slip.

13. Even on a day when I feel weak and feel that I am attacked, You, Lord, hold me steady. You always lead me to a place of safety, for You delight in me. <u>Psalm 18: 25 The Book</u> On the day when I was weakest, they attacked. But the Lord held me steady. He led me to a place of safety, for He delights in me.

14. I have strength for all things, Christ, for You have empowered me. I am ready for anything and equal to anything through You who has infused inner strength into me. I am now self-sufficient in Your sufficiency. <u>Philip. 4:13 AMP</u> I have strength for all things in Christ Who empowers me--I am ready for anything and equal to anything through Him Who infuses inner strength into me, [that is I am self sufficient in Christ's sufficiency].

15. What awe I feel, kneeling before You, for You the God of Israel have given strength and mighty power to me. I bless You, my God. <u>Psalm 68:35 TLB</u> What awe we feel, kneeling here before him in the sanctuary. The God of Israel gives strength and mighty power to his people. Blessed be God!

16. I walk in Your strength, Lord; I tell everyone that You alone are just and good. <u>Psalm 71:16 TLB</u> I walk in the strength of the Lord God. I tell everyone that you alone are just and good.

17. I now have salvation. I now have strength. The kingdom of God has come to me along with Your power, Christ. <u>Revelation 12:10a KJV</u> Now is come salvation, and strength, and the kingdom of our God, and the power of his Christ.

18. Your joy is now in me, Lord and that is my strength. <u>Neh. 8:10b KJV</u> For the joy of the Lord is your strength.

SUCCESS

1. I succeed because You have made me to succeed. <u>Romans 14:4 TEV</u> He shall succeed, because God is able to make him to succeed.

2. Thank You, Jesus, that I am Your sheep and I hear Your voice, and You know me and I follow You. I am in the place where You bless me. <u>John 10:27 KJV</u> My sheep hear my voice, and I know them, and they follow me.

3. You, Lord, are guiding me at all times and satisfy me with all kinds of good things. You keep me healthy, too, so I am like a well-watered garden. <u>Isaiah 58:11 AMP</u> And the Lord will guide you continually, and satisfy you with all good things, and keep you healthy too; and you will be like a well-watered garden, like an ever-flowing spring.

4. You have given me strength and are blessing me with peace. <u>Psalm 29:11 KJV</u> The LORD will give strength unto his people; the LORD will bless his people with peace.

5. Bless You, Lord, for all these benefits You pour on me daily. You are the God of my salvation. <u>Psalm 68:19 KJV</u> Blessed be the Lord, who daily loadeth us with benefits, even the God of our salvation. Selah.

6. You are the light of my world. I follow You so I don't walk in darkness, not knowing what I am doing; instead, I have Your light of life to guide me. <u>John 8:12 KJV</u> Then spake Jesus again unto them, saying, I am the light of the world: he that followeth me shall not walk in darkness, but shall have the light of life.

7. I do not have a spirit of fear, for You have given me a spirit of power, a spirit of love, and a spirit of a sound mind and self-control and discipline. <u>2 Timothy 1:7 AMP</u> For God did not give you a spirit of timidity--of cowardice, of craven and cringing and fawning fear--but [He has given us a spirit] of power and of love and of calm and well-balanced mind and discipline and self control.

8. Thank You that You have quickened me according to everything that You say is mine in the scriptures. <u>Psalm 119:25b KJV</u> Quicken thou me according to thy word.

9. I am prospering in everything I put my hand to for I dwell in the land You have given me. <u>Deut. 28:8b TLB</u> The Lord will prosper everything you do when you arrive in the land the Lord your God is giving you.

10. Lord, You have sent Your angels to be with me and they now prosper my way. <u>Genesis. 24:40a KJV</u> The LORD, will send his angel with thee, and prosper thy way.

Ruth Shinness 2539 E. 450 N Anderson, IN 46012-9518 Web: www.prayerstrategy.com
e-mail PrayerStrategy@juno.com Phone (765) 643-0612 & (765) 642-0623

SUCCESS

11. I speak Your Word and meditate on it day and night, so Your Word is working in me to prosper me and give me good success. Joshua 1:8 KJV This book of the law shall not depart out of thy mouth; but thou shalt meditate therein day and night, that thou mayest observe to do according to all that is written therein: for then thou shalt make thy way prosperous, and then thou shalt have good success.

12. Thank You, Lord, for making perfect everything that concerns me. You do not forsake me, for I am the work of Your hands. Psalm 138:8 KJV The LORD will perfect that which concerneth me: thy mercy, O LORD, endureth forever: forsake not the works of thine own hands.

13. Your favor, Lord, is on me and You have established the work of my hands. Psalm 90:17 NIV May the favor of the Lord our God rest upon us; establish the work of our hands for us--yes, establish the work of our hands.

14. I have risen; I am shining, for You, my light, Jesus, have come and Your glory has risen upon me. Isaiah 60:1 KJV Arise, shine; For thy light has come! And the glory of the LORD is risen upon thee.

15. You love me, Jesus, and give me hope. You comfort my heart, and You have established me in every good word and work. 2 Thes. 2:16-17 NKJV Now may our Lord Jesus Christ Himself, and our God and Father, who has loved us and given us everlasting consolation and good hope by grace, comfort your hearts and establish you in every good word and work.

16. You have plans for me, plans to prosper me and not to harm me, plans to give me hope and a good future. Jeremiah 29:11 NIV "For I know the plans I have for you," declares the LORD, "plans to prosper you and not to harm you, plans to give you hope and a future."

17. You are my Lord, and You teach me what is best for me and lead me in the way I should go. Isaiah 48:17 NIV This is what the LORD says- your Redeemer, the Holy One of Israel: "I am the LORD your God, who teaches you what is best for you, who directs you in the way you should go."

18. Through You, Christ, I can do all things, for You have strengthened me. Philip. 4:13 KJV I can do all things through Christ which strengtheneth me.

19. My success--at which so many stand amazed--is because You are my mighty protector. All the day long, I praise and honor You for all You have done for me. Psalm 71:7 The Book My success--at which so many stand amazed-- is because You are my mighty protector. All day long I'll praise and honor You, O God, for all that You have done.

Ruth Shinness 2539 E. 450 N. Anderson, IN 46012 Web: www.prayerstrategy.com
e-mail PrayerStrategy@juno.com Phone (765) 643-0612 & (765) 642-0623

63

WORK

1. Thank You that You give me the gift of enjoying the good of all my labor. Eccles. 3:13 KJV And also that every man should eat and drink, and enjoy the good of all his labour, it is the gift of God.

2. Thank You, Lord, that Your favor is on me and You have established the work of my hands. Psalm 90:17 NIV May the favor of the Lord our God rest upon us, establish the work of our hands for us--yes, establish the work of our hands.

3. I am doing the good work You have planned ahead of time for me to do. Ephes. 2:10 NIV For we are God's workmanship, created in Christ Jesus to do good works, which God prepared in advance for us to do.

4. God, You have worked Your good purpose in me, both to desire to do my work and to get it done. Philip. 2:13 NIV For it is God who works in you to will and to act according to his good purpose.

5. You have given me hope and You comfort my heart and have established me in every good word and work. 2 Thes. 2:16 KJV Now our Lord Jesus Christ himself, comfort your hearts, and stablish you in every good word and work.

6. Thank You, Lord, for giving me favor and success. You have made me a leader in all I do. Psalm 90:17 TLB And let the Lord our God favor us and give us success. May he give permanence to all we do.

7. You have commanded a blessing on all the work that I set my hand to do in the land You have given me. Deut. 28:8 KJV The LORD shall command the blessing upon thee in thy storehouses, and in all that thou settest thine hand unto; and he shall bless thee in the land which the LORD thy God giveth thee.

8. I succeed in my work because You have made me to succeed. Romans 14:4 TEV He shall succeed, because God is able to make him to succeed.

9. I make plans on how to do my work, Lord, but I count on You to direct my way. Proverbs 16:9 TLB We should make plans--counting on God to direct us.

10. I have nothing to fear about how my work turns out, for You have not given me a spirit of fear. You have given me a spirit of power, a sound mind, self-control and discipline, so I do a good job. I also have a spirit of love so I am able to bless all I work with. 2 Timothy 1:7 AMP For God did not give you a spirit of timidity--of cowardice, of craven and cringing and fawning fear--but [He has given us a spirit] of power and of love and of calm and well-balanced mind and discipline and self-control.

Ruth Shinness 2539 E. 450 N Anderson, IN 46012-9518 Web: www.prayerstrategy.com
e-mail PrayerStrategy@juno.com Phone (765) 643-0612 & (765) 642-0623

WORK

11. Lord, I believe that You have worked a good work in and through me and that You have now helped me to complete it. Philip. 1:6 TLB And I am sure that God who began the good work within you will keep right on helping you grow in his grace until his task within you is finally finished on that day when Jesus Christ returns.

12. I do not become weary of doing my work well, for I am reaping a blessing and a harvest. Galatians 6:9 NIV Let us not become weary in doing good, for at the proper time we will reap a harvest if we do not give up.

13. You have granted me my request: You have wonderfully blessed me and helped me in my work. You are with me in all that I do and have kept me from evil and disaster. 1 Chron. 4:10b The Book (Jabez Prayer) "Oh, that you would wonderfully bless me and help me in all my work; please be with me in all that I do, and keep me from evil and disaster." And God granted him his request.

14. I enjoy my work and accept my lot in life, for that is Your gift to Me, God. I don't look back with sorrow about my past, for You have given me joy. Eccles. 5:20 TLB To enjoy your work and to accept your lot in life--that is indeed a gift from God. The person who does that will not need to look back with sorrow on his past, for God gives him joy.

15. My work brings me profit. Proverbs 14:23 The Book Work brings profit.

16. My hard work returns many blessings to me. Proverbs 12:14b The Book And hard work returns many blessings to him.

17. Thank You that I hear Your voice when I do my work, for You give me inspiration and tell me "This is the way," and whether to go to the left or right. Isaiah 30:21 KJV And thine ears shall hear a word behind thee, saying, This *is* the way, walk ye in it, when ye turn to the right hand, and when ye turn to the left.

18. I am working hard with gladness all the time, as though working for You, Christ. I do Your will with all my heart. You pay me for the good things I do. Ephes. 6:7-9 The Book Work hard with gladness all the time, as though working for Christ, doing the will of God with all your hearts Remember the Lord will pay you.

19. Thank You, Lord, that You have given me a mind to work. Neh. 4:6b KJV For the people had a mind to work.

20. I am strong when I work, for You, God, are with me. Haggai 2:4 b KJV Be strong, all ye people of the land, saith the Lord, and work: for I am with you, saith the Lord of host.

VICTORY OVER THE ENEMY

1. In these days, no weapon formed against me succeeds, and I have justice against every lie; for this is my heritage. This is the blessing You have given me, for I am Your servant. Isaiah 54:17 TLB But in that coming day, no weapon turned against you shall succeed, and you will have justice against every courtroom lie. This is the heritage of the servants of the Lord. This is the blessing I have given you," says the Lord.

2. I have nothing to fear, for You, Lord, are with me. I do not look around with terror, and I am not dismayed, for You are my God. You have strengthened me to difficulties. Yes, You are helping me, holding me up and retaining me with Your victorious right hand of rightness and justice. Isaiah 41:10 AMP Fear not [there is nothing to fear], for I am with you; do not look around in terror and be dismayed, for I am your God. I will strengthen and harden you to difficulties, yes, I will help you; yes I will hold you up and retain you with my [victorious] right hand of rightness and justice.

3. I hide myself in You, Lord, and You protect me from trouble while You surround me with songs of deliverance. You instruct me and teach me in the way I should go. You counsel me and watch over me. Psalm 32:7-8 NIV You are my hiding place; you will protect me from trouble and surround me with songs of deliverance. I will instruct you and teach you in the way you should go; I will counsel you and watch over you.

4. God, You always cause me to triumph in Christ. 2 Corth. 2:14a KJV Now thanks be unto God, which always causeth us to triumph in Christ.

5. I no longer have my mind on the enemy, but stay my mind on You and Your Word. Isaiah 10:20 KJV And it shall come to pass in that day, that the remnant of Israel, and such as are escaped of the house of Jacob, shall no more again stay upon him that smote them; but shall stay upon the LORD, the Holy One of Israel, in truth.

6. Lord, You have preserved me from all evil. Psalm 121:7 KJV The LORD shall preserve thee from all evil: he shall preserve thy soul.

7. I love You, Lord, for You have heard my prayers and answered them. Psalm 116:1 TLB I love the Lord because he hears my prayers and answers them.

8. Thank You, God, You have given me the victory through my Lord Jesus Christ. 1 Corth. 15:57 KJV But thanks *be* to God, which giveth us the victory through our Lord Jesus Christ.

Ruth Shinness 2539 E. 450 N Anderson, IN 46012-9518 Web: www.prayerstrategy.com
e-mail PrayerStrategy@juno.com Phone (765) 643-0612 & (765) 642-0623

VICTORY OVER THE ENEMY

9. You, Lord, are my strength. You teach my hands to war. You are my goodness, my fortress, my high tower, my deliverer, my shield; and in You, I put my trust. You subdue the people under me. Psalms 144:1-2 KJV Blessed be the LORD my strength, which teacheth my hands to war, and my fingers to fight: My goodness, and my fortress; my high tower, and my deliverer; my shield, and he in whom I trust; who subdueth my people under me.

10. My adversaries are clothed with shame and they cover themselves with their own confusion. Psalm 109:29 KJV Let mine adversaries be clothed with shame, and let them cover themselves with their own confusion, as with a mantle.

11. You have delivered me from wicked and evil men who are not believers. 2 Thes. 3:2 NIV And pray that we may be delivered from wicked and evil men, for not everyone has faith.

12. You have made perfect everything that concerns me, for I am the work of Your hands. Psalm 138:8 KJV The LORD will perfect that which concerneth me: thy mercy, O LORD, endureth forever: forsake not the works of thine own hands.

13. Your angels have camped all around me and have delivered me. Psalm 34:7 NKJV The angel of the LORD encamps all around those who fear Him, And delivers them.

14. Lord, I trust in You alone and enemies do not defeat me. You rescue me because You always do right. Psalm 31:1 TLB Lord, I trust in you alone. Don't let my enemies defeat me. Rescue me because you are the God who always does what is right.

15. I am not afraid of the battle ahead, for the battle is not mine, but Yours, God. I need not fight, but stand still and see that Your salvation is now with me. 2 Chron. 20:15b,17a KJV Be not afraid nor dismayed by reason of this great multitude; for the battle is not yours, but God's. Ye shall not need to fight in this battle: set yourselves, stand ye still, and see the salvation of the LORD with you.

16. God, You said, "I will never fail you nor forsake you." So I say without fear or doubt, "You, Lord, are my helper, I am not afraid of anything that mere man can do to me." Hebrews 13:5a-6 TLB God has said, "I will never, never fail you nor forsake you." That is why we can say without any doubt or fear, "The Lord is my Helper, and I am not afraid of anything that mere man can do to me."

17. I make my ways to please You, God, so now my worst enemies are at peace with me. Proverbs 16:7 TLB When a man is trying to please God, God makes even his worst enemies to be at peace with him.

WOMAN

1. I am a capable, intelligent and virtuous woman, and my husband finds me to be far more precious than jewels, and my value is far above rubies or pearls. Proverbs 31:10 NIV A wife of noble character who can find? She is worth far more than rubies.

2. My husband trusts in me, so he has no lack of gain. Proverbs 31:11 NKJV The heart of her husband safely trusts her; So he will have no lack of gain.

3. I comfort, encourage and do him good as long as there is life in me. Proverbs 31:12 AMP She will comfort, encourage and do him only good as long as there is life within her.

4. I open my hand to the poor and needy, whether in body, mind or spirit. Proverbs 31:20 NKJV She extends her hand to the poor, Yes, she reaches out her hands to the needy.

5. My husband is known, for he is successful in everything he puts his hand to. He sits among the elders of the land. Proverbs 31:23 AMP Her husband is known in the city's gates, when he sits among the elders of the land. Deut. 28:8a KJV The Lord shall command a blessing on thee and thy storehouses, and all that thy settest thy hand unto.

6. Strength and dignity are my clothing, and my position is strong and secure. Lord, You cause me to rejoice in the time to come. Proverbs 31:25 KJV Strength and honour are her clothing; and she shall rejoice in time to come.

7. I open my mouth with skillful and godly wisdom and in my tongue is the law of kindness--giving counsel and instruction. Proverbs 31:26 AMP She opens her mouth with skillful and godly Wisdom, and in her tongue is the law of kindness – giving counsel and instruction.

8. I look well to my household and eat not the bread of idleness, gossip, discontent or self-pity. Proverbs 31:27 AMP She looks well to how things go in her household, and the bread of idleness [gossip, discontent, and self-pity] she will not eat.

9. My children rise up and call me blessed; my husband does, too; and he praises me with these words, "There are many fine women in the world, but You are the best of them all." Proverbs 31:28-29 The Book Her children stand up and bless her: so does her husband. He praises her with these words: "There are many fine women in the world, but you are the best of them all!"

10. I am a wise woman who builds her home to be a blessing. Proverbs 14:1 KJV Every wise woman buildeth her house: but the foolish plucketh it down with her hands.

Ruth Shinness 2539 E. 450 N Anderson, IN 46012-9518 Web: www.prayerstrategy.com
e-mail PrayerStrategy@juno.com Phone (765) 643-0612 & (765) 642-0623

WOMAN

11. I fear and reverence You, God, so I am greatly praised. Proverbs 31:30 KJV Favour is deceitful, and beauty is vain: but a woman that feareth the LORD, she shall be praised.

12. I am praised for the fine things I do. These good deeds of mine bring me honor and recognition from even the leaders of the nations. Proverbs 31:31 TLB Praise her for the many fine things she does. These good deeds of hers shall bring her honor and recognition from even the leaders of nations.

13. I am strong, for I choose to joy in You, Lord. Neh. 8:10 KJV For the joy of the LORD is your strength.

14. I respect and reverence my husband. I notice him, regard him, honor him, prefer him, venerate him, esteem him; and I defer to him, praise him; and love him and admire him exceedingly. Ephes. 5:33b AMP Let the wife see that she respects and reverences her husband-that she notices him, regards him, honors him, prefers him, venerates and esteems him; and that she defers to him, praises him, and loves and admires him exceedingly.

15. I fit in with my husband's plans; for if he refuses to listen when I talk to him about the Lord, he will be won by my respectful behavior. My godly life will speak to him more than words. 1 Peter 3:1 TLB Wives, fit in with your husbands' plans; for then if they refuse to listen to them when you talk to them about the Lord, they will be won by your respectful, pure behavior. Your godly lives will speak to them better than any words.

16. I am beautiful inside, in my heart, with the lasting charm of a gentle, quiet spirit that is so precious to You, God, just like the women of old who trusted You and fitted in with their husband's plans. 1 Peter 3:4-5 TLB Be beautiful inside, in your hearts, with the lasting charm of a gentle and quiet spirit that is so precious to God. That kind of deep beauty was seen in the saintly women of old, who trusted God and fitted in with their husbands' plans.

17. The light in my eyes rejoices the hearts of my family, friends, and co-workers, and my good news nourishes the bones. Proverbs 15:30 AMP The light in the eyes [of him whose heart is joyful] rejoices the heart of others, and good news nourishes the bones.

18. My happy heart does everyone good like a medicine, and my cheerful mind heals those around me. Proverbs 17:22a AMP A happy heart is good medicine and a cheerful mind works healing.

DELIVERANCE SOLUTIONS

1. Now is the day Jesus, that You have taken the burden from off my shoulder and the yoke from off my neck, and the yoke has been destroyed because of Your anointing that is upon me. Isaiah 10:27 KJV And it shall come to pass in that day, *that* his burden shall be taken away from off thy shoulder, and his yoke from off thy neck, and the yoke shall be destroyed because of the anointing.

2. My eyes are always toward You, Lord, and now You have plucked my feet out of the net. Psalm 25:15 KJV Mine eyes *are* ever toward the LORD; for he shall pluck my feet out of the net.

3. You have kept my soul and delivered me, O Lord; I am not ashamed, for I have put my trust in You. Psalm 25:20 KJV O keep my soul, and deliver me: let me not be ashamed; for I put my trust in thee.

4. My life was full of ups and downs and my soul was melted because of trouble. I was at my wit's ends. Then I cried unto You, Lord, and You brought me out of my distresses. The storms in my life are now calm and the waves are stilled. Psalm 107:26-29 KJV They mount up to the heaven, they go down again to the depths: their soul is melted because of trouble. They reel to and fro, and stagger like a drunken man, and are at their wit's end. Then they cry unto the LORD in their trouble, and he bringeth them out of their distresses. He maketh the storm a calm, so that the waves thereof are still.

5. Thank You, Jesus, for coming to earth to destroy the works of the devil that had plagued my life. 1 John 3:8b KJV For this purpose the Son of God was manifested, that he might destroy the works of the devil.

6. By Your Word, Lord, I have been kept from the path of the destroyer. Psalm 17:4b KJV By the word of thy lips I have kept *me from* the paths of the destroyer.

7. Lord, You are holding me by Your right hand, and You say to me, Don't be afraid; for You are now with me to help me. Isaiah 41:13 TLB I am holding you by your right hand--I, the Lord your God--and I say to you, Don't be afraid; I am here to help you.

8. God, You have rescued me from dead-end alleys and dark dungeons. You have set me up in the kingdom of the Son You love so much, the Son who got me out of the pit I was in and got rid of the sins I was doomed to keep repeating. Col. 1:13-14 God rescued us from dead-end alleys and dark dungeons. He's set us up in the kingdom of the Son he loves so much, the Son who got us out of the pit we were in, got rid of the sins we were doomed to keep repeating.

Ruth Shinness 2539 E. 450 N Anderson, IN 46012-9518 Web: www.prayerstrategy.com
e-mail PrayerStrategy@juno.com Phone (765) 643-0612 & (765) 642-0623

GOD'S HEART FOR ISRAEL

1. I agree with You, Lord, I too pray for the peace of Jerusalem, and because I love and pray for this nation, I prosper. <u>Psalm 122:6 KJV</u> Pray for the peace of Jerusalem: they shall prosper that love thee.

2. Lord, I proclaim that You who scattered Israel now gather them and You watch over this flock like a shepherd, having redeemed them from the hand of those who were too strong for them. <u>Jeremiah 31:10,11 NIV</u> "Hear the word of the LORD, O nations; proclaim it in distant coastlands: 'He who scattered Israel will gather them and will watch over his flock like a shepherd.' For the LORD will ransom Jacob and redeem them from the hand of those stronger than they.

3. Jesus, You have come and Israel is delivered and saved from their sins. <u>Romans 11:26 MES</u> "A champion will stride down from the mountain of Zion; he'll clean house in Jacob. And this is my commitment to my people: removal of sins."

4. You have taken out the stony heart of sin and given them a new heart of love, and put a new spirit within them so that they obey Your laws and do whatever You command. <u>Ezekiel 36:26-27 TLB</u> And I will give you a new heart--I will give you new and right desires--and put a new spirit within you. I will take out your stony hearts of sin and give you new hearts of love. And I will put my Spirit within you so that you will obey my laws and do whatever I command.

5. They have come and are shouting for joy on the heights of Zion. They are radiant with joy over Your goodness—the grain, the new wine and the oil, the young flocks and herds. They are like a well-watered garden, and sorrow is gone from them. <u>Jeremiah 31:12 NIV</u> They will come and shout for joy on the heights of Zion; they will rejoice in the bounty of the LORD--the grain, the new wine and the oil, the young of the flocks and herds. They will be like a well-watered garden, and they will sorrow no more.

6. Israel is no longer called Forsaken and neither is their land called Desolate, for now, Lord, You call them Hephzi-bah, which means You delight in them. You now call their land Beulah, for their land is now married, owned and protected by You, Lord. Thank You that their new name is Sought Out. <u>Isaiah 62:4,12 KJV</u> Thou shalt no more be termed Forsaken; neither shall thy land any more be termed Desolate: but thou shalt be called Hephzi-bah, and thy land Beulah: for the LORD delighteth in thee, and thy land shall be married. And they shall call them, The holy people, The redeemed of the LORD: and thou shalt be called, Sought out, A city not forsaken.

7. Your love and mercy for Israel will last forever. <u>Ezra 3:11b The Book</u> "He is good, and his love and mercy toward Israel will last forever."

Ruth Shinness 2539 E. 450 N. Anderson, IN 46012 Web: www.prayerstrategy.com
e-mail <u>PrayerStrategy@juno.com</u> Phone (765) 643-0612 & (765) 642-0623

71

PRAYER STRATEGY WORKS IN KENYA

During the month of Feb. 1996, God gave me a word through a prophet who came to our city saying that 1996 was a year for God to release me to the Nations and that meet with God's ordained people who would visit my church in Africa and make a difference in the church.

I had the opportunity to visit the USA between June and September of 1996. I attended a convention in Ashland, Virginia, and one night I heard a voice telling me that I would meet a great man of God who would visit my church in Africa and bless my people, making a difference in the church. It would be a person God had put a teaching in their heart on prayer.

The following morning, very early indeed, I heard the same voice wake me up and tell me to go for a walk and you would meet the man. I obeyed the voice, dressed and walked down the road.

As I went, I didn't see any big man, but a little woman out walking. I just greeted her and walked farther down to meet the man. Surprisingly, I didn't meet any man down the road. Could it be the little woman I met? But that was a poor little woman and the voice said a great man. I expected to meet a very wealthy man who could build us our church and give us the money we needed. God's ways are not man's ways and He is no respecter of persons. He can use the weak vessels for his glory as it is not by power or might.

The whole day I stayed a very troubled and confused person. However, through the guidance of the Holy Spirit, during lunch break, I went to the dining room, got my plate of food and walked to the table. The person who came and sat next to me was Ruth Shinness, the same little woman who I saw walking that morning. We introduced ourselves and we talked about our ministries. She told me about her Prayer Scripture Book, and the Holy Spirit told me to invite her to my church in Kenya to teach prayer. God also appeared to me in vision and showed me that the woman I met was the great one He had shown me.

Our God also had provided another opportunity for me to go to the USA to do business for the mayor of our city, and the business was for only a few days. I was given a ticket for the whole month and the rest of the days I went and met Sister Ruth Shinness who had problems with her pastor on whether to let her come. They didn't know me and he was concerned for her security

God made it possible for me to visit and meet with her pastor who was then very positive about her coming to Kenya. God's purpose will always be accomplished no matter how much the cost.

We planned for Ruth to visit us for the Easter Convention 1997 and stay for two weeks.

Our church by then was experiencing all kinds of problems. Only four of the fifty people in our church had jobs. There was no money to pay for the building. There was no electricity in the church, and church members had all kinds of sicknesses and demonic possessions. Everything was so difficult and we had all kinds of problems.

My church is prayerful, fasting and praying Monday and Tuesday, praying all night Friday and people praying around the clock other times, but we were not getting results to our prayers. We learned that we were not using the right methods to get answers.

Ruth taught us that our God is a God of covenant, and what He has said, He will do through His Word.

Ruth gave us books and tapes on praying Scriptures, and we started using them.

Ruth Shinness 2539 E. 450 N Anderson, IN 46012-9518 Web: www.prayerstrategy.com
e-mail PrayerStrategy@juno.com Phone (765) 643-0612 & (765) 642-0623

We also had another Seminar-Crusade at another small town, Busia, in a village near the Uganda border. A church was planted after the Crusade with Ruth, and the people of the new church also learned to pray the Scriptures. The church has planted another eleven churches and five in Uganda without foreign support and all because of using these prayer strategies.

Great doors have opened for me [the Bishop] and the other members of the church. We started getting breakthroughs in our lives. Members became mature and more responsible to the church, and they started tithing more than ever before. The offering rose to ten times, and every Sunday new people came to church.

Hatred and disunity were gone and members started working together in unity and greater love than ever before. The saints started getting employment and there was joy peace and love in their homes. There was provision and many in the church started to get out of debt.

Our church doubled in size and offerings went up. There was more anointing power and more of God in the ministry. We got equipment we needed for the ministry. Many members got jobs and others started small businesses that are more paying. They live a happy and blessed life. There is joy in the church every Sunday and we are always late in going home because of the anointing. Many things have happened since then and there are signs of greater doors to open.

Testimonies From Kenya

Mary Wanjiru, a member of the church, was jobless and her husband was a building contractor who lost his job. They were in stress and had a totally difficult life. Most of the time they got food from my house and friends. God blessed her with a good job, and her husband started getting big building contracts. They live a happy life and even moved to a bigger house. They are now good tithers and are a blessing to the needy ones in the church.

Tabitha Wangare had nightmares at night. She heard people knocking her utensils and walking in her house every night after she went to bed. She had sleepless nights and was seriously affected in her health. Her business was running poorly, and really living a strenuous life. Sometimes she felt as if she was being strangled by the neck as she went to bed, and her neck was swollen the following day. She would see ugly people (devils) staring at her and was scared. She moved from house to house but this didn't help until one day I led her through the *Prayer Strategy Resource Book*, and let her confess through the Scriptures, and all her problems came to an end. She was late the following morning going to work as she slept so soundly that night. She has never had nightmares since then and her business picked up to excellent. She is now a happy beautiful girl. Before she looked very old with a very scary face. She now looks younger and beautiful.

Charles Wangan was a casual laborer with the council of Nakuru, Kenya. He started praying the way Ruth taught and he got a very big promotion to a clerk, and is now a supervisor over 200 water billing clerks in the same council. He has led ten other clerks in the department to our church, and they are now active members.

Peter Njguna is a motor vehicle mechanic and he hardly had any customers. People didn't take vehicles to him for repairs. He had problems at home for food, school fees and house rent. Most of the time the church helped him, as he is an elder in the church. He started

Ruth Shinness 2539 E. 450 N. Anderson, IN 46012 Web: www.prayerstrategy.com
e-mail PrayerStrategy@juno.com Phone (765) 643-0612 & (765) 642-0623

73

praying using Scriptures and now other mechanics are jealous of him as vehicles are lined up waiting to be attended by him. He moved to a bigger house, and all his children go to the best schools.

I (Ruth) also got another testimony from Africa from Gordon Snow, who is a well-known singer from Kenya. He traveled with us during the Crusades. He said he listened closely to my talks and prayed the Success and Prosperity pages, among others. His dream was to own a recording studio and now he does and it is a success. I have heard he has also started a church.

A pastor who came to the Crusade in Nakuru, Kenya wrote to say he didn't know any of the people at the church where the Crusade was held, but was given a Prayer Strategy Resource Book. (We gave the book to every pastor who came.) He started to pray the book and follow the principles of giving, and soon he had enough money to be able to pay to come to the U.S. and pay his own way to bible school.

We stayed at the mayor's house in Nakuru, and met Emily the house girl who helped us. She had memorized much of the *Prayer Strategy Resource Book* while were there. We heard from her the next summer when she wrote that her mother had been in the hospital, in a coma with malaria and was not expected to live.

Emily would sit by her bed and read aloud the prayers from the Prayer Strategy Resource book. Her mother soon rose up healed.

Victory Over the Enemy

My friend Sue gave her son-in-law Vaughn the 'Victory Over the Enemy' page from my *Prayer Strategy Resource Book*. He had been disabled in an accident and had been trying to get disability for several years, with no success.

He prayed the 'Victory Over The Enemy' page, praying it twice a day.

One day, a crisis occurred in his situation and he, being upset, called Sue. Her advice was, "Get Ruth's prayer page and pray it until you get some peace." About the third time through it, he felt great joy, as the presence of the Lord came upon him.

When he went to church on Sunday, he got up to tell about it, and that same joyous presence came over the whole church, and they had a revival that morning.

The next week a state legislator took up his case. It was soon settled, and he received retroactive pay.

South Bend Prayer Group

One autumn, I spoke to a prayer group in South Bend, Indiana. They are very structured and organized, and people call them with prayer requests. After I spoke there, they would look through my book for one or two scriptural prayers for each concern, and each member would pray that for the following week.

The next spring, they sent a letter telling the answers. One was about four people with an alcohol problem who after six months are now dry and recovering. (2 Corth. 2:5:17-19)

Three divorced mothers regained and/or retained visitation privileges and custody of the children. (Isaiah 54:17 and Daniel 1:9.)

Two scriptures helped four persons to obtain jobs or promotions. (Romans 14:4 and Psalm 138:8.)

Ruth Shinness 2539 E. 450 N Anderson, IN 46012-9518 Web: www.prayerstrategy.com
e-mail PrayerStrategy@juno.com Phone (765) 643-0612 & (765) 642-0623

Praying (Psalm 118:16-17) has seen three people successfully through bone marrow transplants, two through heart surgeries, and another through pneumonia complicated by heart problems.

Using Scripture (Deut. 28:4) we have seen the delivery of seven healthy babies (one set of twins). Three of the pregnancies were fraught with difficulties, bleeding problems, dehydration, premature labor, one a potential for Down's Syndrome, which included much medical intervention. All the babies are perfect and beautiful.

Forgiving and Blessing

I made this page because I had a problem forgiving someone I loved very much. I would think and hurt about it day and night. I would tell people that Prayer Strategy works for everything, so I set out to see if it would really work for this.

As I made up the Forgiving and Blessing page I noticed how often the word "blessing" appeared, so I would pray the page and also a blessing for that person often during the day. I was soon set free of the unforgiveness. Sometimes it would want to sneak back, so then I would go back to the prayer page and the blessing again. It works!

Work Page

One of my children had been working on a music CD for about three years. He promised to have it finished in two months for a special event. It seemed impossible. I made up a "Work" prayer page for him and sent it to each member of his family. They all prayed. He was anointed with creative ideas. Sometimes he would work sixteen hours at a time. He thought it was the best CD he had ever done. He was enabled by the power of God to finish the good work he had started.

Since then I have successfully used the "Work" page myself, bringing some of my dreams into reality.

Woman In Depression

I had spoken in a church in Muncie. One woman who had suffered depression for years and was having an extra hard time, had bought my Prayer Strategy book. Her mind was so troubled that she started to pray my book to help her to keep her mind focused and away from the confused thoughts.

She continued this steadily for a whole week. Toward the end of the week the Spirit of the Lord came down on her and set her free of depression.

That Sunday she shared at church, and the Lord came down on the whole congregation and people rushed to the altar.

A Family Prospers Through Prayer

I was a little skeptical about praying the "Prosper" Scriptures as if I already had the answer, and actually were receiving wealth. Maybe other people received money this way, but I was sure I never would.

First, I had to repent of my attitude. Of course, the Lord wanted me to prosper!

After applying the principles of praying Scriptures as if I already had the answer, checks started arriving in the mail! First $45, and then $98, $160, and $200! Next came a check for $5,800.

My husband and I had been working on a business deal for two years. We felt we had been beating our heads against the wall. The Lord stepped in and we saved $34,000 dollars on the transaction!

Are my husband and I super slick business people? No! We serve an awesome God! God is so good--all the time!

An Indiana Family Set Free

In March of 1996, Ruth put a Scripture book together for my family and me. At that time, my son had drifted away from the Lord. He was deep into satanic mischief and deeply depressed.

My husband was a substance abuser. His dependence on drugs had increased to the point of using drugs several times a day.

I was at the end of my rope, scared for my loved ones, and felt abandoned by God.

After applying the principles of praying Scriptures as if I already had the answer, my family began to change dramatically.

My son rededicated his life to the Lord that same month and has been serving Jesus ever since.

Two months later my husband ended a twenty-year drug addiction. Now three years later, he is still drug free. Praise the Lord!

Free Form Mental Illness

One lady reports that she had, for many years, been to doctors, counselors, and on heavy medication because of mental illness. Nothing seemed to help. She was on disability. She got this book, and because she had plenty of time, she spent long hours praying these prayers. She reports that she is now free from her problems of the mind and is at last normal.

Success At Last

This man is a hard working Christian, but he never seemed to reach his expectations for all the good work and long hours he put in. There were continual disappointments along the way of his life. His wife would always say, "If there is a lousy job to have, you will find it." He got what she said. She then started praying the *Prayer Strategy Resource Book*, saying what God says he has.

That scenario has now turned around. He has favor and honor at his work, his company gave him a free trip to Hawaii and his company supplied him with a new vehicle, free gas for his work and pleasure.

The son had followed in the footsteps of his Dad as a failure, had a verbally abusive wife who left him, but now he is married to a lovely Christian wife who loves him unconditionally. He was promoted to boss of his company, so he supports her well.

Results of "Go-Ye" and "Bringing Unity" Scriptures

What a joy it has been praying these scriptures and watching God do great things in all areas of our lives! Just since I have been praying the "Go-Ye" scriptures, my husband and I have both become involved in bringing people to Christ. In the last 4 months, we've seen 29 souls saved.

By praying the "Bringing Unity" scriptures, God has wonderfully changed the spirit of our home and marriage. We now enjoy a beautiful, loving, heaven-on-earth relationship where the sweet Spirit of Jesus is sensed.

Mother Saved

I just wanted to let you know the wonderful thing that happened Palm Sunday. The day after you had your "Unlocking the Heavens Seminar, at South Meridian Church of God,

76

Ruth Shinness 2539 E. 450 N Anderson, IN 46012-9518 Web: www.prayerstrategy.com
e-mail PrayerStrategy@juno.com Phone (765) 643-0612 & (765) 642-0623

my Mother was very near death, and we were worried because she was not a Christian. Whenever I was with her, she would never commit her life to Christ. I went home that evening after the meeting and started praying the Mother page in the *Miracle-Grow Family Prayer Book*. The next day was Palm Sunday and I asked Myrna Fox if she would go and pray with Mom. Myrna did on Mom's 94th birthday; she gave her heart to the Lord. Praise the Lord for all His Glory!

Testimonies From Russia

Our Prayer Team leader's daughter (she is 15 years of age) began to pray "Healing" page out of your *Prayer Strategy resource Book* and she got rid of a serious problem with her spine so quickly that the doctor was amazed, he couldn't believe that it was possible.

Nina: I also have a wonderful testimony from my personal life. I asked God to open a door for me to do interpreting for missionaries, not only twice a year for ten days but on a constant basis, though it seemed to be absolutely impossible. I used to work as a tutor in the last two years and usually in the fall people would phone to invite me to teach their children. But that fall nobody phoned, yet I didn't have any desire to look for pupils and was full of joy, had perfect peace and kept on just thanking God. In the end of September a pastor from one church phoned to ask me to interpret for a girl missionary named Erika who had just come to Samara to start a Bible School. Since then we have been working together for a year and two months. It was one of the happiest periods in my life. Many anointed men and women of God come to teach in the Bible School and to preach in local churches. It was amazing! We enjoy every moment of our work together and I have become a real friend with Erika. Different people told me that when she was speaking with me interpreting it seemed to them that the two of us were like one person speaking. Besides Bible School classes four times a week and Sunday services we also used to go to a great many of cell groups. Some people come for prayer or for counseling we have wonderful prayer meetings and prayer nights, youth meetings, meetings with different pastors. Often we work from early morning till late night. But doing this I feel that for me it's not just a way to earn money but it's a ministry from God. I feel myself in God's perfect will and it's an amazing feeling!

Nickoli: "When I was already a Christian it happened that my business (Smoked Fish) was not successful any more, so I made a lot of debts. To pay all the debts I was to give my house and my fish-smoking business to my creditors but even then I would still owe them a lot. If I would compare it with my present income I would have to be paying that debt my whole life. They have very much power and each one of them had their own illegal "military units." They used to take everything from those who owed them with no compassion.

For a long time it had been my dream to get your prayer book. At first you gave me your pages in English (in Good News church). I tried to have them translated but that translator asked so much money that I was not able to pay ($1000). But later your Prayer Strategy Resource Book had been published in Russian.

I prayed the following pages-"Fear Not," "Strength," "Victory Over the Enemy". In addition to that I used your strategy to pick Scriptures that I needed in my situation, "Protection," "Delivered from Enemy's Hands," "Blessings for the Righteous."

God delivered me in the very last moment. I already had all the papers ready for my house to be given over to them. Even now I don't understand what happened. But for one and a half years they have not been bothering me any more. Praise the Lord!

Ruth Shinness 2539 E. 450 N. Anderson, IN 46012 Web: www.prayerstrategy.com
e-mail PrayerStrategy@juno.com Phone (765) 643-0612 & (765) 642-0623

77

Poleena: "My daughter was divorced and very unhappy. I began to pray Family page and God told me that everything will change. Some time later God gave her a wonderful husband; they really love one another. Now they have a newly born daughter. I trust that they will serve the Lord together because I see that my daughter has begun to listen with interest when I tell her about God.

We also used to pray "My Pastor," "My Church" page and we see that God blesses them more and more. The church is growing in number; new young people come to the church. Children Sunday school is growing, we had a wonderful Bible School this spring and fall.

Singapore: Testimony of Joyce Seow: I have been using the prayer strategy book for over a year. However, in January 2004 I reminded Abba Father, about my finances. You see, I am self-employed and have a business of my own since 1991 but with economic slowdown, SARS, Bird Flu etc like everywhere else the industry has sluggish.

After praying the Prosper page, Abba said, Daughter the projects will come, but in areas that you least expect". I said okay Abba and rested in His love.

In February I had a call from a long time friend who rang to ask if I still have my business. I said yes, and he promptly recommended that I call a particular 5 Star heritage hotel in Singapore. I got the project after the first interview with the General Manager. Even as she was talking to me, I heard Abba say, " My favour makes a circle about you like a shield."

After the first phone call, a project that I was working on for close to a year finally concluded. And the party that had the franchise decided not to go with it and gave the whole thing over to me to run. This is clearly the Lord.

Since I have been using the Prayer Strategy Resource Book by Ruth Shinness, I have been walking in victory and my walk with the Lord Jesus Christ has never been the same.

Philippines: In 2003, Vee A. Natividad, owner of "International Freight Forwarding and Shipping Agency" in the Philippines, lost a big customer and at the same time two of her top employees quit.

In August she received the Prayer Strategy Resource Book from her friend Joyce Seow in Singapore. Vee would go to her church, World For Christ Fellowship Church in Manilla, open to the Favor and Prosper pages and read each prayer in a loud voice, declaring the favor, blessings, and prosperity for her life and that of her business.

In several months the Lord sent proper replacements for both job openings.

On January 2004, she successfully negotiated a new shipping account bigger than the one she lost. And from that date on God has added numbers of new business opportunities. One being a new company she opened with partnership with a company based in China, with a new office in China. She was invited to be a stock holder for a natural gas drilling company in the Philippines.

The Pre-School at the World For Christ Fellowship Church received an upgraded accreditation from Dept. of Education for the next level. (grade 1 to 6).

Because of the guidance through Prayer Strategy Resource Book, Vee has now formed a new company called V-PowerAct Intl. Inc. in partnership with Joyce Seow from Singapore. They are planning to print the books in the Philippines with vision and mission that all Filipino people will receive the book and be blessed and delivered from poverty.

Ruth Shinness 2539 E. 450 N Anderson, IN 46012-9518 Web: www.prayerstrategy.com
e-mail PrayerStrategy@juno.com Phone (765) 643-0612 & (765) 642-0623